BOOMERANG
KIDS

A REVEALING LOOK AT WHY
SO MANY OF OUR CHILDREN
ARE FAILING ON THEIR OWN,
AND HOW PARENTS CAN HELP

CARL PICKHARDT, PhD

D1111922

sourcebooks

Published by Sourcebooks, Inc.
P.O. Box 4410, Naperville, Illinois 60567-4410
(630) 961-3900
Fax: (630) 961-2168
www.sourcebooks.com

Library of Congress Cataloging-in-Publication Data

Pickhardt, Carl E.
  Boomerang kids : a revealing look at why so many of our children are failing on their own, and how parents can help / Carl Pickhardt.
      p. cm.
  Includes bibliographical references and index.
  1. Parent and adult child. 2. Young adults—Psychology. 3. Adulthood—Psychological aspects. 4. Parenting. I. Title.
  HQ755.86.P53 2011
  155.6'5—dc22

                                   2011010334

              Printed and bound in the United States of America.
                VP 10 9 8 7 6 5 4 3 2 1

Also by Carl Pickhardt, PhD

Why Good Kids Act Cruel: The Hidden
Truth about the Pre-Teen Years

Stop the Screaming: How to Turn Angry Conflict
with Your Child into Positive Communication

The Future of Your Only Child: How to Guide
Your Child to a Happy and Successful Life

The Connected Father: Understanding Your Unique Role
and Responsibilities during Your Child's Adolescence

To all those parents whose son or daughter comes home after foundering for independence and needs help to recover and get ready to try again.

"It ain't over till it's over."

—*Yogi Berra*

DISCLAIMER

Unless otherwise attributed, all quotations and examples in this book are fictional, made up by me to illustrate psychological points similar in kind but not in actuality to cases I have known.

CONTENTS

INTRODUCTION

"I figured I was ready to move out and make it on my own. I had a little money saved, a job lined up, a place with a couple of roommates to stay where we could share expenses. But it just got away from me. Maybe it was too much, too fast, I don't know. For a lot of reasons I just couldn't catch hold. I crashed. And when you crash in life, where else are you supposed to go except back home? Disappointed? Sure, I'm disappointed. And so are my parents, though they don't come out and say so. I just need a safe place and some time to get my feet back under me so I can try moving out on my own again."

For many parents, hearing from their child how hard it is striking out alone in the world is difficult, even heartbreaking. But the reality is that such stories are becoming more and more common.

Today, the adolescent journey from childhood to adult independence is a long one, and the hardest part is usually saved for last. This final stage of adolescence, what I call trial independence, typically unfolds between the ages of eighteen and twenty-three and ends a little after the college-age years, when a young person finally establishes social, psychological, and economic independence.

The problem, though, is that most parents and adolescents have been led to believe that graduation from high school signifies that one is ready to act self-sufficiently and responsibly grown-up. This assumption is reinforced by many of our books, television shows, movies…even our laws. For most older adolescents today, it normally takes at least three to five years after high school, when they are living away from home and struggling to operate more on their own, to actually master the skills needed for independent living. And most adults (and most young people themselves) vastly underestimate the complexity of this final struggle for independence. This miscalculation becomes most apparent when it results in boomerang kids—last-stage adolescents who lose their footing and come back home to rely on their parents' support for a while longer.

I have written this book to help parents understand this last and most challenging stage of adolescence, the one in which most boomerang kids tend to return to reside at home. By understanding the nature of this challenging time and identifying the multiple causes for returning home, parents can move past frustration and instead focus on helping their child move on to adulthood.

Hopefully, this book will help you understand *why* your son or daughter has returned, *what* you can do to support your child's recovery, and *how* to strengthen your child's readiness and resolve to try for independence again. So what I have written is primarily a manual for *intervention* when your last-stage adolescent returns home; but it is also a guide for *prevention*, since it discusses how you can prepare children before they depart from the home, making a boomerang return less likely.

Chapter 1 describes the last stage of adolescence—trial independence—setting it within the context of four stages of normal adolescent development. Chapter 2 examines how immaturity or delayed development from earlier adolescent stages can put off readiness for independence, and how adequate preparation before the child's departure from home can increase the chances of a successful launch.

Chapters 3–13 walk you step by step through the main life challenges encountered during trial independence. When one or more of the following challenges comes to the point of crisis, it can cause a young person to boomerang home to recover:

- *Missing home and family*—coping with loneliness after moving out on one's own
- *Managing increased freedom*—handling a greater range of choice
- *Flunking out of college*—failing to complete further education
- *Unemployment*—seeking or losing a job
- *Roommate problems*—sharing a domestic living arrangement
- *Broken love relationships*—finding and losing love
- *Substance use*—living in a drug-filled world
- *Indebtedness*—overspending and credit card living

- *Stress*—coping with excessive demand
- *Emotional crisis*—feeling overwhelmed by unhappy feelings
- *Fear of the future*—facing what to do with one's life

By understanding these challenges and how to help children navigate through them, parents can learn how best to ready children before they leave or support them after they return home.

Chapter 14 makes recommendations for how parents and boomerang kids can structure this period of residence so that it works as well as possible for all concerned. Chapter 15 describes the gifts available to young people in each type of crisis, and how these gifts can help them grow. Finally, Chapter 16 describes how to recognize the end of adolescence, identifies some developmental tasks of young adulthood that follow, and recommends how parents can adjust their parenting to stay well connected to their grown son or daughter during the independent years ahead.

At the end of each chapter, I give a "Parenting Prescription," which summarizes several actions that parents can take and topics for them to discuss that can be helpful to their son or daughter at this trying time of life.

My hope is that this book will help parents in three ways:

1. Give you a road map to normal life challenges your son or daughter will face during trial independence (age 18–23) and the final stage of adolescence, as well as an appreciation of why this last of the four stages is typically the hardest of all

2. Describe eleven major life challenges that most young people commonly encounter during this final stage, and how those challenges can come to crisis and cause a young person to return home

3. Suggest ways you can support your child's recovery in each crisis and help lead the young person closer to adulthood, readier to try independence again

Most of what I have to share about understanding and managing boomerang behavior in older adolescents arises from counseling parents and young people over the years. From this experience, I have come to believe that this is a trying time for all concerned. Parents who thought their active parenting was over now have more to do. The young person feels that returning home is necessary, but wishes that this wasn't so. Sometimes mothers and fathers will wonder if they shouldn't be out of the parenting business by this age, but in general, I think not. Just as adolescence often lasts longer today than it used to, active parenting must last longer, too. When a young person boomerangs home during trial independence, this simply means that he or she has more growing to do. This book describes how parents can be there to help.

CHAPTER ONE

THE LAST STAGE
OF ADOLESCENCE

"She's 22 years old, for heaven's sake! We thought she'd be grown up by now. But no, it's one more crisis after another. And then she calls on us— for emotional support, problem-solving advice. Even money...although we've gotten pretty tough about that. It's like she's still a teen! Why is it so hard for her just to act like an adult?"

In the United States, between the ages of eighteen and twenty-three, most older adolescents expect, and are expected, to move out and try to live on their own—maybe sharing an apartment with friends or in some cases with roommates at college.

This is not the case everywhere. At a talk I gave several years ago, a parent from South America stood up and said: "Why do you want your children to grow up, leave home, and live independent of family? In my country, you are expected to grow up, stay home, and become a contributing part of the multigenerational family who all help each other. Why do you want your grown children to go away? Why do you want to break up the family?"

This is true: young people are not obliged to leave home any more than parents are obliged to have them go. And multi-generational families can be healthy, happy, and productive places in which grown-up young people can live. But the reality is that in our culture, the majority of young people in the final stage of adolescence (and their parents) believe that it's time to move out, so they can be themselves, live on their own terms, and be responsible for their own care. Yet, despite trying hard to do so, many young people falter.

So how do we help them understand themselves and the challenges they face so that they can succeed at living on their own and growing fully into adulthood?

To begin, we need a firm understanding of the adolescent years, how they affect both children and parents, and how they build toward independence. Thus, in this chapter, we will closely examine the following:

- The first three stages of adolescence
- Stage four: trial independence
- Necessary parental adjustments during trial independence

THE FIRST THREE STAGES OF ADOLESCENCE

When they think of adolescence, most people commonly think of the middle school through high school years (or children age 12–18).

However, adolescence actually begins in late elementary school (usually starting around age 9–13) and doesn't end until the early to mid-twenties. Adolescence typically lasts about ten to twelve years. During this time, young people work to gather sufficient knowledge, experience, and self-reliance to forsake the supports of childhood, to gain more responsibility, to develop a more mature sense of identity, and to learn to manage life independently. This journey to independence through the teenage years is a labored one, because trial, error, and recovery are the halting steps required for growing up. Progress and backsliding go hand in hand.

For young people and their parents, the process can seem unpredictable, creating a certain amount of anxiety for all concerned. It's like the shortsighted leading the blind. Parents are shortsighted because most of what they know about growing up comes from their own adolescent experience, which was at a previous time, in a different family system, and under social circumstances that are no longer in place. Young people are blind because everything is new to them, and they feel anxious and excited about the discoveries to be made, freedoms to be gained, and new adventures to be had.

For parents, there is more worry than excitement. They often feel they have no option but ignorance as the turbulent teenage years unfold, but this is not true. You don't have to be governed by confusion, ignorance, and surprise during the teenage years. You can be informed.

Look for Your Own Denial

The first step in understanding your child's adolescence is honestly remembering your own and overcoming your own denial about what growing up was really like. The parents I meet who seem to have the most difficulty adjusting when their engaging child transforms into a more abrasive adolescent are those who suffer from three specific types of denial:

1. "What happens with other people's children in adolescence won't happen to mine."
2. "I didn't do dumb or wild stuff in my adolescence, so my child shouldn't either."
3. "Adolescence is different today from when I was growing up, so my teenager won't have to go through what I did."

Denial is the enemy in hiding. It keeps parents from acknowledging the truth of what did happen, what is happening, or what may happen to their teenager.

Come adolescence, it's best for parents to face the alterations of adolescence head-on. This means accepting that some unwelcome changes will happen to their child during adolescence. This means admitting that, just as they acted out, experienced hard times, and messed up while going through their own teenage years, their son or daughter will do some of the same. This means understanding how, from one generation to the next, although the social context is not the same as it was in the parents' youth, the basics of the adolescent experience haven't changed that much.

So how do you know if you are in denial? I have developed twenty-five points (originally published in my book *The Connected Father*) that will help you recognize denial. During your own adolescence, do you remember any of the following?

1. Wanting your parents to stop treating you as a child
2. Thinking your parents didn't understand you or were unfair
3. Arguing more with your parents and resenting their authority
4. Wanting to be more private and to talk to your parents less
5. Becoming more preoccupied with your personal appearance and dress
6. Not liking the way you looked
7. Feeling unpopular for not having friends or all the friends you wanted
8. Testing, getting around, and beating the adult system
9. Putting off parental requests and breaking parental rules
10. Wanting to stay up later at night and sleep in later in the morning
11. Not working hard at school or working just hard enough to get by
12. Keeping your parents from finding out what was going on
13. Sneaking out after your parents were asleep
14. Getting into more fights with your parents
15. Lying to parents to do the forbidden or to get out of trouble
16. Shoplifting or stealing to see what you could get away with
17. Daring to do something risky, escaping injury, or getting hurt

18. Wanting to spend more time with friends than with family
19. Experimenting with tobacco, alcohol, or other drugs
20. Becoming more interested in sex
21. Hating boredom and loving excitement
22. Going along with the group when that really wasn't what you wanted to do
23. Making impulsive decisions that you later had cause to regret
24. Wanting to engage in adult activities before you were grown-up
25. Doing something illegal to get the freedom you desired

If you answered no to many of these questions, then you may be in parental denial. If you answered yes to many of these questions, then you can now better understand how little adolescence has changed and that many of the ways you felt, believed, and behaved back then, your teenagers will probably feel and think and act now.

So before you explode at your teenager in anger or surprise—"You did what? How could you do such a thing?"—take the time to ask yourself if, while growing up, you ever did something similar. Parents shouldn't do this to excuse their children, but to see if they can relate to them, their situation, and their state of mind. Instead of getting mad, think of how different it would be to say:

"I never exactly got into this kind of trouble, but I came close on a couple of occasions, so I can remember what that was like. The main thing for you to understand is that there isn't much you can

get into now that I couldn't get into, or didn't know about, back when I was growing up. So let's talk about how you feel, what you learned, and what needs to happen now."

Understanding the First Three Stages

Although the teenage years involve a lot of uncertainty, the progression of a young person's development, and the parenting challenges that it creates, are generally consistent. That is, certain changes, conflicts, and problems tend to unfold in a somewhat orderly progression. If you can anticipate the likelihood of these changes and events, you are more likely to react rationally, not emotionally. An emotional reaction can end up making a hard situation worse. So what follows is an abbreviated road map to adolescent change, a framework based on my observations from counseling young people and their parents over the years.

When parents know what to anticipate, they can ease their response to normal bumps along the way and not be surprised by these unwelcome turns of events. They can respond to changes effectively and not overreact. The best way to keep up with teenagers is to stay ahead. So, let's take a look at the normal challenges in each of the first three stages of adolescence.

STAGE 1: EARLY ADOLESCENCE (AGE 9–13)

In early adolescence, the main challenge is separation from childhood. Early adolescents cast off childhood by rejecting their old family identity and the role of being a child. In loosening ties of dependency on parents and lessening communication with them, young people become more interested in the larger world beyond the shelter of family, a world they are now more eager to explore. At this time, young people bridle more against parental demands and restraints and develop a more negative mind-set toward parents and toward themselves, while parents mourn the loss of the adoring and adorable little child they will never have again.

Problems that parents encounter at this stage are typically characterized by the following changes in young people:

- *A negative attitude*—Adolescents are increasingly unhappy with being defined and treated as children. They know how they don't want to be but haven't yet figured out how they do want to be. They are less interested in traditional childhood activities, and they grow bored, restless, and frustrated from not knowing what else to do. They have a growing sense of grievance about unfair demands and limits that adults in general, and parents in particular, impose on their daily freedom. More dissatisfaction and complaints become the order of the day. This negative attitude provides the child's motivation to change from child into someone older.

- *Active and passive resistance*—Adolescents question rules more and delay responses to parental requests. In the process, young people can let normal home and school responsibilities go, in an effort to live more on their own terms and less on the terms set by adult authority. Now a ten-minute task can drag on for several hours, and adolescents will take endless issue with whatever parents have to say. More delay and argument become the order of the day. This active and passive rebellion emerges to develop the child's power to change.

- *Early experimentation*—With more power of resistance established, young people begin to test limits and rules more to see which are truly fixed and which are flexible, to see what they must obey and what they can get away with. What rules do parents really mean? What rules are they willing to back up? What rules do they consistently enforce? Testing social limits at this age can include such activities as shoplifting, vandalizing, making prank calls, and experimenting with substances like cigarettes, alcohol, inhalants, and other drugs. Adolescents become more frightened and fascinated by the dark and dangerous possibilities that lurk in the larger world. More curiosity and interest in the forbidden becomes the order of the day. This early experimentation develops the child's experience of change.

STAGE 2: MID-ADOLESCENCE (AGE 13–15)

In mid-adolescence, the main challenge is to begin forming a family of friends. Those friends will support and accompany (and pressure) the young person through the experiences and adventures of growing up. Your child will tell his or her friends much more about what is going on than he or she will tell you. Mid-adolescents are more inclined to keep you in ignorance and even deceive you to protect their privacy and enable their freedom of action. At this time, teenagers are more determined than ever to fight parents for the social independence that they believe is necessary to have time and keep up with their friends.

Parenting problems encountered at this stage are typically characterized by the following changes in the adolescent:

- *Increased disagreement*—Where early adolescents were prepared to argue about restrictions, mid-adolescents are prepared to mount more intense opposition to adult authority. Personal freedom is no longer just an issue of principle to debate but a matter of extreme practical importance. They feel a social urgency to be out in the actual world in the company of adventurous friends, but parents must be persuaded first. There is a tyranny of "now": "If you don't let me go, my life will be ruined!" Opposition is meant to move parents out of the way. Parents can feel that they are in a thankless position as they take unpopular stands for their children's best interests and are resented for those efforts. More conflict with, and disapproval from, teenagers is the order of the day.
- *Lying*—Young people lie to protect their freedom, to escape consequences, and to get to do what has been forbidden. They are aware that you depend on them for reliable information about their activities, and so they are more tempted to exploit that dependency by lying. They not only tell you less than the whole truth but also tell more untruths. The

teenager believes that parents are best kept in the dark. More deception to keep parents in ignorance becomes the order of the day.

- *Social belonging*—Because young people at this age know that adolescence is no time to go it alone, group membership assumes great importance. Acts of social cruelty—teasing, exclusion, bullying, spreading rumors, ganging up—become more common as young people jockey for social standing and place during a time when it is harder to socially get along. Maintaining good social standing with one's friends becomes key to keeping one's place in this vital company. To do so, teenagers must give up some personal freedom. The adolescent chooses conformity to fit in and social compliance to go along. To violate either set of demands by appearing too different or too independent risks criticism or even being cast out by the group. Social membership at this age is not free. More peer pressure is the order of the day.

STAGE 3: LATE ADOLESCENCE (AGE 15–18)

In late adolescence, the main challenge is for teens to *act more grown-up*. These are the high school years. Although both parents and teenager are in agreement about the need for the teen to act more grown-up, they have very different definitions about what that actually means. For parents, acting more grown-up is about exercising more adult responsibility. For the late adolescent, acting more grown-up is about having "adult" adventures. In addition, the young person has growing excitement and anxiety about approaching independence. The young person does not feel fully prepared to manage the separation from home and to shoulder the responsibilities that will soon come with living more on his or her own.

Parenting problems encountered at this age are typically characterized by the following changes in the late adolescent:

- *Seeking status*—Teens desire to engage in certifiably grown-up activities, such as part-time employment (making their own money), driving a car (the freedom machine), dating (having a boyfriend or girlfriend), sexual experiences (acting like a "man" or "woman," according to their perceptions), and recreational drinking or using other drugs at parties (social substance use). The desire is to approximate adulthood by being more on one's own and by trying out behaviors that are associated with being adult (but not always with adult responsibility). Riskier actions and older appearances are the order of the day.

- *Romantic attachment*—When casual dating in high school ignites infatuation, serious dating can also result. If love attachments begin to grow, sexual involvement is more likely to occur. Physical intimacy causes the young relationship to become more emotionally intense. As time together becomes more of a priority, some social isolation from friends results, often arousing conflicts over how much togetherness and separateness, jealousy and possessiveness, the couple can manage. The course of first love is usually more troubled than adolescents expect. More serious relationships are the order of the day.

- *Acute ambivalence*—Young people, on the threshold of the independence they say they have always wanted, discover that part of them doesn't want it at all—leaving family, leaving friends, and leaving the security of familiar surroundings. They lose old companions and feel nervous about their readiness to step off and function apart from family. The harsh realities of operating on one's own start to challenge the ideal fantasy of independence. More separation anxiety about leaving home is the order of the day.

Finishing the First Three Stages

By the time your child has finished the first three stages of adolescence, what has he or she accomplished?

- In early adolescence, your child was successfully able to separate from childhood.
- In mid-adolescence, your child was able to create an independent world of social companions.
- In late adolescence, your child gathered enough experience acting grown-up to desire and dare stepping off on his or her own.

Once these stages are complete, young people feel more ready than not to try putting all that they have learned into practice, to move out on their own. But that does not mean that their adolescence has ended. They are now simply moving on to stage 4, trial independence—the stage when many boomerang kids are born.

STAGE 4: TRIAL INDEPENDENCE (AGE 18–23)

No matter how difficult the earlier teen years may seem, the trial independence stage is usually the hardest for older adolescents, who must now spread their wings and keep their footing at the same time. The young person is likely living away from home for the first time (usually with roommates), either working at a job or pursuing further education or both. Although equipped with the desire for independence, the young person often does not possess all the necessary skills to handle it. Trial independence demands more responsibility than most young people can handle, at least right away. As one young person in the midst of money troubles exclaimed to her parents: "But I've never budgeted, paid bills, or had a bank account before!"

Consider how the demands of trial independence can pile up:

- There's so much freedom, and it is the young person's choice how much to take.
- There's so much responsibility, and it depends on the young person to manage it.
- There's so much social distraction, and it is up to the young person to decide how much to let the good times roll.

- Among their cohort of friends, few seem to have clear direction in life, and many are slipping and sliding and breaking commitments, to their detriment. There are broken romantic relationships, broken job obligations, broken credit arrangements, broken leases, broken educational programs, and even broken laws.

In the extreme, what young people discover, usually at some cost, is that assuming responsible independence is more difficult than they anticipated: *"No one told me it would be like this!"* In addition, they may have no clear direction in life, no job path into the future that they want to follow. *"I don't know what I want to do with my life!"* is the rallying cry of the age. Not only that, when they do know what they need to do, they end up at war with themselves. *"I can't make myself get it done!"* is the frustration that many feel. Anxieties abound in the face of challenges that often feel overwhelming and diminish confidence and self-esteem: *"What's the matter with me?"*

Then, they must also cope with the effects of an unhealthy lifestyle. Many young people in this stage do not take good care of themselves, as power of want triumphs over power of will, as impulse overrules judgment, and as temptation overcomes restraint. They suffer from sleep deprivation; poor dietary habits; procrastination; debt from credit spending; nonstop socializing; maximum availability of alcohol and other drugs; and low self-esteem from feeling developmentally incompetent and unable to get their lives together at such an advanced age.

In consequence, many young people in this last stage are subject to a great variation of unhappy emotions. They may experience despondency, loneliness, stress, confusion, uncertainty, insecurity, disappointment, guilt, shame, anxiety, and exhaustion, for example, and they may resort to substances to escape these feelings and manage their discomfort. The three to five years after high school can be a period of extremely heavy and varied substance use, which disorganizes the lives of many young people at this vulnerable age. Unprotected by family, young people in this stage are more exposed to sharers and sellers of illicit drugs. So if your child gets into serious difficulty from poor judgment during trial independence, always assess the role of substance use in the unfolding of unhappy events. If there had been no drinking or other substance using, would he or she have made the same choices?

All young people will encounter their own unique set of challenges during trial independence. But when you are committed, engaged, settled down, and practical, it can be hard to empathize with a child in his or her early twenties who is uncommitted, disengaged, unsettled, and unrealistic. Plus, with your declining influence, lack of information, and dread that your child might make life-harming decisions, it is easy to feel frightened and to let fear be you guide. But constantly showing worry, impatience, or criticism will only make matters worse for your older adolescent, who is riddled by those same hard emotions themselves.

Instead, you must work to show respect for their right and responsibility to make decisions, confidence in your child's capacity to make sound decisions and to learn from mistakes, and support for him or her to keep on trying to make independence work. This is the time to change the focus of your parenting, a time to stop *managing* your child and to provide *mentoring* instead. The next section describes how to make this shift.

HOW PARENTING MUST CHANGE

Just because young people are on their own (or trying to be) doesn't mean that they don't still need their parents to be involved. In fact, because of the significant challenges that come with trial independence, children need parents more than ever before. Parents are needed, however, in a different way. In this last stage of adolescence, it is essential that parents change their role from being *managers* (imposing supervision and regulation) to becoming *mentors* (offering consultation and advice—when asked).

If you barge in and try to control an adolescent's troubled life at this late stage (when a job has been lost and bills are past due), you risk rescuing your child from learning the life lessons that facing consequences and taking responsibility have to teach. If you are quick to criticize mistakes and shortcomings, you also risk estranging yourself from your child and reducing communication with a child who refuses to be censured anymore. As one angry young person declared: "I would rather have nothing to do with them than hear what they have to say or have to do what they say! It's my life, and they need to get used to it!" But, of course, when she returns home to recover from a crisis, she invites them back into her life to a degree by depending on their care.

To become a mentor, parents have to shift position in relation to their son or daughter. Up until now, parents have had a managerial, *vertical relationship*, where authority placed them in a superior or dominant position, from which they evaluated conduct, directed behavior, and dictated terms of living from above. In trial independence, however, young people do not welcome and usually will not tolerate being judged, directed, or having terms of living dictated by parents. In response, they may pull away and communicate less to parents who treat them in these old, controlling ways.

So to maintain a workable connection at this time, when this connection is sorely needed, parents need to establish a mentoring, *horizontal relationship*, where there is more equity between them, and parents live alongside their children on terms of mutual respect. The mentoring contract states that the parents will respect the young person's right and responsibility to make independent decisions, and the young person will respect the wisdom of life experience the parents can offer.

Mentoring needs to be a consensual, consultative, and collaborative relationship where, by invitation only, parents help with problem solving, sharing what experiences and ideas they have to offer, and being objective and never evaluative. "Based on the difficulty you describe, this is how you might want to choose your way out of this problem. Of course, this is your life, you know it best, and the decision is entirely up to you." The parents who have the hardest time shifting from a vertical (managerial) to a horizontal (mentoring) relationship tend to be authoritarian. They want to control, they know best, they are always right, they will be in charge, and they insist on getting their way.

To effectively enact this new parenting role, you must let go of all corrective discipline. You neither criticize nor punish. If you want your young person to come to you and learn from you, you must forsake all expressions of frustration and disapproval, disappointment and worry, impatience and anger. You must respect the young person's right to make her own decisions, even when you do not agree with those decisions. You are no longer in the business of trying to control or determine choices by bending the conduct of your child's life to your will. Facing real-world consequences will provide discipline enough. You need to empathize, encourage, and advise or coach when asked.

How can you tell the difference between managing and mentoring?

- Managing parents dominate from above as authorities; mentoring parents consult from alongside as collaborators.
- Managing parents give unsolicited directives; mentoring parents offer advice only if asked.
- Managing parents hold on; mentoring parents let go.
- Managing parents are hands-on; mentoring parents are hands-off.
- Managing parents jump in; mentoring parents keep out.
- Managing parents mind the young person's business; mentoring parents consider the young person's life his or her business.

- Managing parents set the young person's agenda; mentoring parents expect the young person to set an agenda of his or her own.
- Managing parents are evaluative; mentoring parents are nonjudgmental.
- Managing parents lecture; mentoring parents listen.
- Managing parents direct; mentoring parents suggest.
- Managing parents rescue; mentoring parents support self-help.

The mentoring rule is, *Accept before advising.* If parents cannot accept a young person's right to independent choice without the respect that acceptance conveys, then the young person will feel disapproval or criticism and will wall him- or herself off from the parents for self-protection. Parental acceptance opens the door for parental advice to get in. Now young people are more likely to be open to parental counsel because they know that their parents have no censure to offer, only their knowledge, experience, and problem-solving help.

Many adolescents in this last stage before young adulthood lose their independent footing and must be encouraged to learn after the fact, from sad experience, what they did not learn before. They must learn the hard way, by making mistakes and taking responsibility for their recovery. Even mature adolescents can lose their footing in trial independence, because maturity cannot make up for inexperience. The job of parents, through mentoring, is to support their child's will to keep on trying and to be accessible so that he or she can benefit from the experience and understanding that parents have to offer.

As mentors, your role is not to tell young people what to do or to "make" them do anything. Your role is not to bail them out of difficulty. Your role is not to express disappointment, criticism, frustration, anger, worry, or despair. Instead, listen empathetically; advise if asked; let go of any responsibility for fixing whatever is going wrong; and offer faith that young people, having chosen their way into trouble, have what it takes to choose their way out.

Obviously, the willingness of a young person to come to you when confused, undecided, in need of counsel, or in difficulty depends on there being comfortable and trustful communication. To that end, you must not evaluate or interfere, and you must be affirmative, constant, and loving. Being an effective mentor means being emotionally approachable. Mentors express

- faith, not doubt ("You can do it");
- patience, not anger ("Keep after it");
- consultation, not criticism ("You might try this");
- understanding, not disappointment ("It's hard to manage independence"); and
- confidence, not worry ("You have what it takes!").

If you do provide help, do so only after you see evidence of self-help in your child first. And be cautious about the amount of help you give, because the downside of any help is that it protracts dependency—the young person depends on you to do what he is unable or unwilling to do for himself. For example, if you help a college student with projects or papers just as you did when she was in high school, it may enhance her performance, but it will disable her independence.

All the while, you must be aware of your child's self-esteem. There is a major drop in self-esteem during trial independence, a painful sense of developmental incompetence: "I'm old enough to be adult, but I keep messing up!" If you hear this from your son or daughter, you can say, "Most young people don't find their independent footing without first making some slips, because there are so many new responsibilities to learn and so many new commitments to keep." As a mentor, experienced with your own trial-and-error education, let your son or daughter know that mistakes are a foundation for learning throughout everyone's life.

In fact, one of the most important parts of being a mentoring parent is to encourage learning through mistakes. In childhood, the age of dependence, a conscientious parent is often the best teacher. In the last stage of adolescence, confrontation with hard consequences from poor choices is usually the best teacher.

Trial, error, and recovery mark the adolescent learning curve of growing up. This can be hard for parents to accept. The older their children grow the less tolerant parents typically become when errors occur. A two-year-old's mistake is easier to accept than a twelve-year-old's mistake, and a twenty-two-year-old's mistake can be frustrating for a parent who expects more maturity. (But remember, because the last stage of adolescence is the hardest—and involves coming to grips with responsible independence—that you should anticipate mistakes from your child during this time.)

Unfortunately, sometimes parents who wish to protect their teenagers will intervene to prevent this invaluable instruction. They will intervene to get them out of trouble; they will quash consequences; and by doing so, they lose an opportunity for education. "He didn't mean to," "She promised never to do it again," "He just wasn't thinking," and "She's really a good kid, so give her a break." In the long run, this kind of parental help can really hurt.

It's better to support mistake-based education and let young people encounter the errors of their ways. For example, consider some of these reasons not to rescue. By dealing with the consequences of

- doing wrong, the adolescent learns to act right;
- forgetting a promise, the adolescent learns to remember commitments;
- breaking a law, the adolescent learns to become more law abiding;
- escaping work and failing, the adolescent learns to bear down and succeed;
- yielding to peer pressure, the adolescent learns to think and act more independently;
- indulging immediate gratification, the adolescent learns to resist temptation;
- getting drunk, the adolescent learns to remain sober;
- lying, the adolescent learns to be honest;
- amassing credit card debt, the adolescent learns not to overspend; and

- procrastinating, the adolescent learns to meet commitments in a more timely way.

To support this after-the-fact instruction, parents not only need to act tough enough to let consequences happen but also need to honor learning the hard way. One of the best ways to do this is to talk about "the great school of life":

"In the great school of life, you and I will never graduate. We'll always be students because we'll never experience it all. We'll never know it all. We'll never master it all. We'll never pay enough attention. We'll never be careful enough. We'll never remember all we should. We'll never get it all right. We'll all do some foolish things. And neither one of us will get all A's. The best we can do is try our best, keep trying when the going gets hard, learn from the errors of our ways, and credit ourselves for doing what works out well. I may not have made your mistakes growing up, but I sure made a bunch of my own. I still do. And I always will."

One father put it well when his twentysomething adolescent was in despair over messing up once again. "Son," the man said, "as far as I'm concerned, if you're not making mistakes in life that just means you're not trying hard enough." And with that opinion, or blessing, a father lifted a world of self-recrimination off the shoulders of his beleaguered son.

The sign of a parent who is a successful mentor to a son or daughter struggling through challenges of trial independence is the ability to help put mistake-based education to constructive use. And in trial independence, there is an enormous opportunity for missteps as young people make their way across the minefield of challenges that separates the last stage of adolescence from entry into young adulthood.

PARENTING PRESCRIPTION

1. Do not expect your adolescent to leave home and enter trial independence completely ready to responsibly assume all the demands of self-sufficiency. There will be more trial and error to do while growing up, and your child might need to return home for a period to recover after failing to master some of the hard challenges of independence.

2. Change your parenting role from being manager of how your son or daughter conducts life (supervising, imposing structure, and setting limits) to becoming a mentor—being willing to share your more mature life experience and advice, if asked, in an accepting and nonjudgmental manner.

3. Be patient with youthful misadventures and mistakes, and be supportive of the important life lessons they can teach. Don't interfere or rescue, but allow your son or daughter to face hard consequences that provide good instruction.

CHAPTER TWO

DELAYED MATURITY

"Maybe it's partly our fault. We always thought of him as our most sensitive child, and so we treated him with special care. Because life just seemed harder for him than the older kids, we made special exceptions for him. We accepted a lot of apologies and promises and gave him a lot of second chances. 'Making excuses,' our older kids called it. They'd say how we were tougher on them and much easier on him. Looking back, they were probably right. For sure, we were always getting him out of scrapes. We'd rush in with help when he acted like he couldn't help himself. Now he's on his third try at college because each previous time he couldn't manage to do the work, although he's certainly smart enough. Of course, we love to see him, but we keep hoping that this time acting grown-up is going to take and that he won't be coming home to live with us again."

Many boomerang kids, sometimes with the complicity of their parents, face the issue of delayed maturity. Although the older adolescent thinks of growing up as gaining more social freedom and independence, parents tend to want something more solid to develop. They call it maturity. By "maturity," parents usually mean that the young person will grow into the fullness of his or her capacities, particularly by assuming responsibility for choices and consequences and coping effectively with the challenges of life.

Explaining the importance of maturity to his departing daughter, a worried dad said: "Maturity allows your best judgment to come out and your best decisions to be made. This means before you make a major decision, check yourself out. Are you seeing the total picture of what is going on now? Are you using all that past experience has to teach? Are you thinking ahead about where your choices might lead?"

The dad wanted his daughter to dethrone impulse and emotion in her decision making and to rely on more judgment and deliberation instead. But how successfully older adolescents navigate trial independence depends a lot on what maturity they learned before they got to this last stage. Specifically, it depends on how they do the following:

- Brave the hard transformations of adolescence
- Choose engagement over escape
- Shoulder "older" responsibilities in high school

In this chapter, we examine each of these topics and explain how not meeting the challenges involved can lead to delayed maturity, which can make trial independence even more difficult.

BRAVING THE TRANSFORMATIONS OF ADOLESCENCE

Adolescence is a painful trade-off: one can't become a more independent adolescent without giving up many benefits of remaining a dependent child.

Once adolescence gets under way, parents will never experience their son or daughter as a little child again. Children will never have their parents as their primary companions again. And the family will not be as harmonious to live in as it once was. That simpler time of closeness and compatibility is over. In addition, young people must face the vast and unknown field of experience outside of family. Because dangers are everywhere, young people's fascination with growing older must contend with fear of worldly dangers ahead.

So the early adolescent has a price to pay—loss of the familiar and anxiety at facing the unknown. This is why adolescents give parents so many double messages:

- "Leave me alone" and "Pay attention to me"
- "Go without me" and "Don't leave me behind"
- "I can do it" and "Do it for me"
- "Don't talk to me" and "You never talk to me"
- "I already know" and "How should I know?"

Which way does the adolescent want it? Both ways—having the freedom of independence and the security of dependence, wanting parents to let go and to hold on, and often at the same time. Daring to forsake the security of depending on parents and to accept the uncertainty of depending more on themselves makes adolescence an act of courage.

In addition, the three developmental engines that drive adolescent development toward independence are frightening as well:

- *Disconnection* creates more distance from parents, with the goal of pulling away from family at home enough to develop one's own independent social "family" of friends, confidants, and companions.
- *Differentiation* creates more incompatibility with parents, with the goal of experimenting with one's individuality and developing one's own unique, independent identity.
- *Disagreement* creates more conflict with parents, with the goal of pushing against parents in order to take more charge of one's own life and to live on more independent terms.

For the young person who is extremely attached to childhood, parents, and family, these changes can be scary. Consider the threatening questions they raise:

- "Will I pull so far away that my connection to my parents and family will be broken?"
- "Will I become so different my parents and family won't accept me?"
- "Will I push so hard against my parents that they will lose their affection for me?"

The more strongly an adolescent is attached to the care of parents and the comforts of childhood, the scarier these questions about adolescent change can become. This can often be the case with an only child or an otherwise specially prized child, for whom parental attachment is so important and for whom parental approval matters so much.

In these cases of high levels of attachment, the relationship with parents can be so bonded, so nurturing, and so pleasurable that it is no wonder that many young people put off the necessary stress of transformation and delay the adolescent process. When they do, however, this means that they will be less mature when it comes time for trial independence. Now adolescent disconnection, differentiation, and disagreement may not begin until early high school.

Holding on is the main issue. Sometimes the child holds on too hard to the old childhood conditions and his or her parents. For example, one thirteen-year-old only child honestly declared to her parents, "I want to grow up, but I want to keep things between us the way they've always been." Sometimes parents hold on too hard to the old conditions of childhood and to their child. For example, there were the parents who wanted to keep protecting and providing for their last adolescent who was left at home, discouraging him from doing things for himself. They thought, "Let us take care of it. Enjoy your childhood while you still can." Sometimes parents and children resist the inevitable separation, thus delaying adolescence: "We have more fun together than we have with anyone else."

The challenge for parents is to stay in communication with their son or daughter while these engines of independence are causing them to grow apart, creating a more abrasive relationship to live in. You must not take adolescence personally, as if it is something your teenager is deliberately doing to offend or injure you. Adolescence is a hard process of growth that a child must dare to do for him- or herself. With this understanding, you must then give your child the following assurance: "No matter how far you pull away from us, no matter how different from us you become, no matter how hard you push against us, you need to know this. Come what may, we will hold you in our loving hearts as we always have and always will."

CHOOSING ENGAGEMENT OVER ESCAPE

"To be or not to be?" is not adolescents' question. Their question is, "To engage or not to engage? To engage or to escape from the onerous demands of life?"

Work or procrastinate, concentrate or space out, confess or lie, show up or skip, stay sober or use substances, respond to daily reality or retreat into electronic entertainment—these are just some of the engage-or-escape choices that adolescents have to face. For the teenager who is mostly concerned with pleasure or comfort, escape from challenge seems like a good short-term strategy. And it is consistent with a pervasive adolescent work ethic: work as hard as you can to get out of doing work (where "work" is what adults want you to do.) But when it comes to growing up, escape proves to be a bad long-term solution. And when parents do not encourage engagement, they can become complicit in the *arrested development* of their child.

Growing up was never made to be easy or to be without hardship. No matter how much fun we have along the way, the challenges are always hard. And hardest of all is this: *only by engaging with these challenges, not escaping from them, can growing up occur.*

Engagement means choosing to grapple with challenges life presents, be they adversities or opportunities, and trying to master them. It also means confronting the outcomes of choices and learning from what those consequences have to teach. With each honest attempt at engagement, successful or not, comes a new measure of responsibility. And increments of responsibility are the building blocks of independence. *Escape is the enemy of responsibility.*

During adolescence, engagement with the challenges of growing up is always in competition with the temptation to escape. But today, the problem is more vexing than ever before because of the age of electronic amusement in which we live. Today's vast world of electronic entertainment offers virtually limitless possibilities for recreational escape. Young people become glued for thirty or forty hours a week (or even more) to television, movies, DVDs, video and computer games, social networking sites, and cell phone texting. Indeed, we have created a culture of escape that, for many young people, is much more tempting to inhabit than one of engagement with the boring or onerous demands of everyday reality. What makes it hard for parents to rein in this escapism is the fact that many parents are equally diverted by electronic entertainment themselves. What parents pursue for themselves, they model and permit for their children.

One of the strongest examples of this is a high school teen whose parents described him as a "lock-in." By that, they meant that their son spent most of his waking hours when not at school confined to his room, attached to his computer and playing endless hours of video games, surfing sites, chatting, and downloading videos. "He's completely content with this life. But what is he going to do next year when he gets to college?" his parents wondered.

This proved to be a good question. The answer turned out to be more of the same. In fact, it was a lot more of the same because of the teen's increased dislocation, loneliness, and anxiety at being out on his own. So in college, the pleasure of electronic escape trumped the effort of attending classes and engaging in schoolwork. He became disengaged from boring studies and invested in fun instead, which led to a drop in his grades. Before he knew it, he was in academic trouble.

Escape is easy. But meeting a challenging demand in life, like performing well in school, builds maturity. It takes paying attention, self-discipline, thoughtful problem solving, a capacity for persistence, a tolerance for boredom and frustration, and the ability to learn from error.

Thus, during the earlier stages of adolescence, it is important for parents to moderate escape activities such as watching TV and movies, playing video games, and using the computer and to encourage active engagement with real-world activities, experiences, and responsibilities. Such engagement comes from activities like the following:

- Job work and volunteer service
- Helping, fixing, and problem solving
- Creative self-expression
- Exercise and conditioning
- Team and organizational membership
- Face-to-face interaction and socializing
- Engaging in physically active play

Each experience of engagement that the adolescent masters becomes one more step on the way to growing up. To excessively indulge in escapes can result in a delayed development of maturity, which in turn can significantly extend the final stage of adolescence. For example, I sometimes counsel a young person who for years has been regularly avoiding what is boring, unpleasant, or taxing by escaping into drug use. Now, in his early twenties, he seems to have the maturity of a fourteen- or fifteen-year-old. At this late age, he has a lot of growing up to do.

SHOULDERING "OLDER" RESPONSIBILITIES IN HIGH SCHOOL

When their adolescent enters high school as a freshman, parents need to ask themselves this question: "Over the next four years, what practical life preparation—knowledge, skills, experience—can we provide so that our teenager has the *smallest next step to independence* when he or she graduates school and leaves our care?" Then parents need to plan and sequence the necessary independence training they will give to empower their child to successfully assume the responsibilities of living away from home.

How can parents provide this training? In three ways: by transferring responsibilities, by teaching exit skills, and by demanding accountability (particularly for "grown-up" behaviors).

- To *transfer responsibilities*, parents can identify what they are doing for their high school freshman that he or she can take responsibility for him- or herself—doing laundry, waking up for school, and preparing meals, for example.

- To *teach exit skills*, parents can identify what basic skills young people need to manage living out in the world, away from home. Parents can make a list of all the skills their child will need to rely on. Then parents can decide when and how they will teach these skills during the four years of high school. For example, young people will need to manage the three B's—banking, bill paying, and budgeting. So when during the high school years will these skills become an integral part of his or her regular responsibilities?

- To *demand accountability*, parents need to recognize that high school is a time when young people try to act more grown-up in many impulsive ways that parents often don't approve of. When unhappy consequences occur (be they from refusal, recklessness, risk taking, or rule breaking) parents need to hold young people accountable for the outcomes of making poor choices. It usually does young people no favors to rescue them from consequences that have an important lesson to teach. Saving a child from trouble now can defer a painful education to a later time, when the consequences may be more severe.

Your goal during the high school years is to increase your adolescent's powers of responsibility so that he or she has the smallest next step toward more self-sufficiency when the time for trial independence arrives.

Ironically, when parents provide the right training, I often hear them complain, "We have done our job of training independent kids too well." What do they mean?

"Both the older kids are in high school, and except for food, health, and shelter, they take complete care of themselves. They're totally responsible, completely self-regulating, making good decisions in all the ways we could want, running their own lives really successfully. The problem is, that doesn't leave much for us to do. They don't need us. Plus, they're so busy taking care of business that they don't have much time for us either. We thought independence would happen after high school. But we've got a junior and a senior living with us who, for all intents and purposes, have already left the nest!"

When parents succeed in training highly independent, mature, and responsible adolescents in high school, they have to a large degree succeeded early in working themselves out of their parenting jobs. But the good news is that their child will have a very small step to take when moving into trial independence.

Now that you have a better understanding of the four stages of adolescence, and how delayed maturity in the earlier stages can arrest your child's growth, it's time to examine eleven common challenges your child will encounter during trial independence. When one or more of these normal challenges comes to crisis, your son or daughter is most likely to boomerang home. The next eleven chapters explain how each crisis can occur.

PARENTING PRESCRIPTION

1. Parents need to tolerate sufficient disconnection, differentiation, and disagreement from their adolescent to allow growth to independence, making it safe to do and seeing it is done within safe and acceptable limits.

2. Parents need to encourage engagement with real-life interactions and demands and to moderate escape into electronic entertainment, which, when excessive, can contribute to arrested development.

3. The parental goal during the first three stages of adolescence should be to encourage the growth of responsibility so that there is the smallest next step to independence when the time arrives to enter the last stage of adolescence, trial independence.

CHAPTER THREE

CHALLENGE #1: MISSING HOME AND FAMILY

"I didn't really want to leave home after graduating high school, and I don't think my parents particularly wanted me to go. But I was eighteen and thought that was the grown-up thing to do. I didn't move far. Just in with a friend and turned my part-time job from senior year into full-time work. But living with a roommate was so cold and lonely. We had different schedules and different friends and didn't see each other that much. Knowing there was all this family activity still going on back home was really hard. I missed being part of it. I missed it terribly, the constant commotion, what was happening in everybody's lives. And when I dropped by to visit, I missed it even more. So that's when I decided to move back home. I just wasn't ready to leave."

With moving out comes the challenge of missing home and family.

For many older adolescents, leaving the comforts, familiarity, routines, companionship, and security of home for the more hardscrabble existence of operating on one's own proves hard to do. In early high school, the time for moving out seems as enticing as the promise of pure freedom. But as graduation approaches, the next step of independent living feels increasingly complicated and daunting to take on. And once young people have moved away, four psychological challenges can make it hard to move past missing home:

1. The demands of change
2. The lifestyle drop
3. The case of homesickness
4. The happy high school experience

Let's examine each of these factors, and how they can be a roadblock to full independence.

THE DEMANDS OF CHANGE

Change is a disruptive process that cuts our ties to what we have grown accustomed to. For young people who have never been away from home before in a significant way, who have lived in one place all their lives, who are strongly attached to family, or who have little experience with major life change, leaving home to live elsewhere can be a major adjustment.

"I didn't realize I'd be uprooting myself," a freshman at a local university explained to me. "Everything I've spent my whole life getting used to has suddenly been torn away. I didn't know it would feel like this! So lonely! Not knowing anyone! Having no place to fit in! So far away from family! It's been hard to sleep, and I haven't felt well. I know it's crazy, but I feel abandoned by my family, when it's me who has left them. It's really hard concentrating on everything that needs to be done here when I spend so much time missing what's back there."

Contrast this young person with another student, a "military brat" for whom going off to the same college has proved no big adjustment. This second student is used to change: "I've been on the move and on my own all my life. Every two years we'd pack up and I was off to a new school. I was just expected to find my way, and I did, making a temporary home wherever I landed. After a while, I got to like the adventure of it. Life was never boring. As a matter of fact, the one thing I'm not sure about myself in college is having to stay put in one place for four long years!"

Getting used to any life change demands adjusting to the loss of the old and engaging with the new. The first can be painful and the second daunting. In combination, these adjustments can create anxieties, and these anxieties express themselves in common worries that parents can often ease.

- *When I leave home, will I be forgotten?* Young people need to know that they are remembered and thought of. By commemorating special occasions and giving expressions of spontaneous caring, parents can let children know that they remain in the family's minds and hearts.

- *When I leave home, will I lose my standing in the family?* Young people need to know that their position in the family is secure. By initially preserving their room and possessions, parents can let them know that their empty room and valued belongings continue to hold their old familiar place.

- *When I leave home, can I still come and stay?* Young people need to know that they are always welcome back. By making a fuss over their visits, parents let them know that they are glad to see them whenever they can.

- *When I leave home, will we still talk?* Young people need to continue communication with the family. By receiving and making calls, parents let their children know the news about what is going on at home.

- *When I leave home, will you still be there if I run into trouble?* Young people need to know that they still have access to family support. Parents should let them know that they are there to help mentor them with any difficulties that may arise.

By addressing these worries affirmatively, parents can provide assurances that encourage adolescents to try for more independence. But sometimes a parent can unwittingly jeopardize a young person's departure by denying one of these five assurances. I am reminded of the father who immediately took over his daughter's empty bedroom, boxed up and moved her belongings into the basement, and turned the vacated space into a study for himself. Now when his daughter came home, she didn't have her old place to stay. Not only that, but all the objects that had meant to so much to her and had marked her history and territory were nowhere in sight. Expressing outrage, the daughter was very frightened and hurt that her presence had been symbolically eradicated in the home, and perhaps in the family. Just because she was ready to leave home didn't mean that she was ready to give up her space at home, so she took the loss as a very painful rejection. Fortunately, her father immediately recognized the error of his ways and put her room back how it was—and how she needed to have it be for a while longer. The lesson is this: when young people physically leave home, they haven't emotionally left home, so retaining that old place is an important way of letting them hold on.

But how long should they hold on for? The reality is that when young people leave to live away from home, it will be many years before they are able to establish a sense of place as powerful as home and relationships as significant as family. In fact, one sign of adulthood is when young people start referring to their independent dwelling, and not the place where their parents live, as "home."

There are other ways parents can add to a young person's difficulty with moving out and staying out. One of the most common is by sending double messages that undercut their adolescent's resolve to move away from home:

- "We want you to be independent, but we're not sure you can make it on your own"—the young person feels a measure of parental *doubt*.

- "We want you to go, even though that means leaving us all alone"—the young person feels torn by a measure of *guilt*.
- "We respect your right to your own decisions, but we can't understand the choices that you've been making"—the young person feels a measure of parental *disapproval*.

When an adolescent is already anxious about leaving, it is best for parents to communicate confidence, not doubt: "We believe that you have what it takes to do this." It is best to express enthusiasm, not instill guilt: "We are excited that you are taking this next step." It is best for parents to give their blessing, not their disapproval: "We think that you have worked really hard for this next opportunity."

By communicating confidence, you will help your child cope with the demands of change and move past his or her feelings of missing home.

THE LIFESTYLE DROP

Another psychological factor that can lead to missing home is when older adolescents face a drop in their standard of living when they are on their own. One young man explained his coming back home this way: "I couldn't afford to live independently. Just the bare necessities were all I had, and it took all I made to pay for those. No car to drive. No cable TV. No cell phone. No computer services. No stocked refrigerator. No bills already paid. It didn't take me long to figure out that I could live better back with my parents than on my own." What he sorely missed were the material comforts of living at home.

For adolescents struggling with a drop in lifestyle, the best thing parents can do is explain the practical principles of starting out in life. They can describe how, when young people leave to live on their own, there is usually a drop in their standard of living. With a part-time or even a full-time job, entry-level employment does not pay much and usually comes with no benefits, such as health insurance, sick leave, or vacation. Young people often have to get used to living on less, both materially and financially, than they did at home.

This point is when important real-world education begins. Part of the challenge of independence is learning to get by on very little, to cut back, to do without, to buy on the cheap, to keep unnecessary expenses down, to stretch a dollar as far as it can go. This is a good time to practice budgeting and learn the self-discipline to keep to a budget. Parents can also share what it was like when they were young and starting out and learning to play the game of getting by on less money. They can also explain how making do with very little motivated them to work hard to be able to be more comfortable.

For some young people, the lifestyle drop that comes with trial independence can be hard to accept if they have been materially indulged and have not had to earn any part of their way during the earlier stages of adolescence. That is all the more reason for parents to give their children early exposure to earning their own way and working for the things they desire. But no matter where parents start, the best way to get past the issue of the drop in lifestyle is to show their child that this challenge—their child's challenge—will help them gain not only the things they want in life but independence as well.

BECOMING HOMESICK

Homesickness feels like a real sickness. It is a combination of grief, anxiety, loneliness, and longing over the loss of family attachments that the separation from home creates. Although homesickness is most common in younger children who are experiencing short-term separation from their family, it can also occur in last-stage adolescents who have moved out for a job or college and find that they terribly miss the security and familiarity they've left behind. When this distance preoccupies a young person, it can significantly interfere with his or her capacity to reach out, get involved in, and adjust to the demands of new surroundings. If social withdrawal and isolation take over, depression can result. Although the pain of homesickness is mostly emotional, it can have bodily expressions, too—aches, nausea, sleeplessness, and general feelings of physical unwellness.

Last-stage adolescents can be complicit in causing their own homesickness when, to affirm their newly won independence, they push parents away, keep them at arm's length, diminish communication to show they do not need it, and cut themselves off from the family connection they miss. Then they can even blame parents for not caring about them, when they are creating their own painful sense of distance by pulling away. A mother in this situation told her daughter, "You can live independently and still stay as much in touch with us as you like. We respect your separate life and we welcome your communication and contact at any time."

A different kind of homesickness grows out of the obligation a young person feels to those left behind, knowing that he or she is missed by those who must now get along without the young person's care. This can also motivate a return home: to shoulder family responsibilities, to tend to a loved one who needs it, to help out family. "My grandmother just wasn't all right with me not there," explained a young woman whose grandparent had been like a second mother.

And sometimes a young person's homesickness is actually a mask for parents' "childsickness." They miss their child terribly and are having a hard time letting go. So they flood her with attention, encumber her with help, and obligate her with need, all to let her know that there is no place like home, no place where she will be more welcome or better loved. In this case, the issue is not simply the young person missing home; it is parents who miss having their child at home. When people talk about "helicopter parents," this hovering attention is usually what they mean.

No matter the cause, homesickness is not a condition to feel guilty about or to criticize. It is simply a reflection of the young person's having a tough time adjusting to the separation from home and the unease of living in a new place.

To work through homesickness, a young person—away at college for example—needs effort and transitional support from parents. If the young person grew up without having many major experiences with short-term separations from home, the separation that accompanies trial independence can be pretty tough. Being able to tolerate separation anxiety, to make an effort to engage with new surroundings, and to build new friendships all take courage and time. Many young people need the transitional support of parental communication, encouragement, and attention during the first year or so living away from home.

The cell phone and computer make these types of connections easy. Call it "electronic weaning" when young people rely on calling, texting, emailing, and messaging with parents while adjusting to more autonomy at the outset. Doing so gives them time to grow their comfort and confidence with their social independence. In these cases, your message needs to be the following:

- "You are not alone."
- "You can call us any time."
- "You can always come back to visit."
- "We support your brave adventure of moving away."

If you faithfully send a message of support, encouragement, and independence, by the second year of living away from home, a familiarity with new surroundings, comfort with new routines, and relationships with new friends usually take hold. Attacks of homesickness become less frequent and severe. The trick is to maintain good contact without interfering, to support autonomy without enabling dependency.

And parents can do one thing more. They can encourage their lonely son or daughter to make *real* connections with real people, and not rely on the Internet to broker new relationships. "When it comes to relationships on the Internet," they can explain, "'friends' are not real friends, how people portray themselves is often not how they really are, and communication is usually devoid of honest emotion. To make satisfying friendships, you need to contact and spend time with people face to face."

THE HAPPY HIGH SCHOOL EXPERIENCE

Sometimes what young people miss is a different kind of home—their high school years. For some, the high school years were the best years of their life, the memory of which makes whatever they encounter next a letdown. In fact, the experience of the high school years can have enormous bearing on how a young person's adjustment to trial independence unfolds. Those students for whom high school was just OK or not great fun may be glad enough when it comes time to graduate. But those students for whom high school was a triumph in every way can have a hard adjustment when they leave.

These students sometimes crash in trial independence because of what I call the curse of the happy high school student. Suppose that in high school you were extremely popular and a superior student, were surrounded by a group of long-standing friends, had a romantically significant boyfriend or girlfriend, and found that many people wanted to get to know you. Then you go away to college, where you are socially no one in particular. With conscientious effort, you get average grades. You have a few acquaintances but no good friends. You have no romantic attachment, and other students show no particular interest in getting to know you. Gone are what seem like the best years of your life. In their place is a time when your old friends have scattered in different directions, and some have lost touch. Your level of achievement in this larger world of competition is relatively modest. What a letdown!

The realization sets in that, comparatively speaking, you will never be as popular or as relatively high achieving as you were in high school. "In high school I was Mr. Somebody!" complained a young man. "Here I'm Mr. Nobody. I was really smart in high school, but here I'm barely average. I looked really good compared with the other guys back home, but here I can't compete with these gym jocks who spend more time lifting weights than they do studying. I wish I could go back to how it was!"

For many young people who leave home, whether moving out with a job or going to college, there is a sense of diminished competency and worth. In the larger world, they will never socially stand out as much or do as well, relatively, as they did in high school. In this more diverse world, they will never fit in so comfortably and securely as they did before. In this less hospitable world, they will have to work harder to create a new social group of friends. And unless they can recalibrate their self-expectations, disappointment and disillusionment may drive them home. When that happens, Mr. Nobody returns to his family at the end of the semester in a funk, with no desire to go back to where he counts for so little. Instead, he is determined to look up all the old high school friends who remain in town, to reconstitute the old group as much as possible, and to resurrect the good times they had as though the past can be recovered—when it actually cannot. For some young people, letting go of high school, and the high point of their life, is a very long good-bye.

After a while, though, even these young people who excelled in high school experience a painful conflict that creates significant discomfort when they hold on to the old high school gang. One young man said: "When I spend time with my old friends, I feel like I'm stalling out. Don't get me wrong. I still love my friends. But I want to move on and move forward with my life, and to do that I have to break out of my circle. And I hate that. I hate having to leave old friends behind!"

His observation was correct. Growing up requires giving up, and one of the hardest parts of home life to give up is letting go of the easy company and constant availability of high school friends. The holding power of these groups slowly erodes away as individual members, one by one, begin a socially independent trajectory in life.

What can help a young person who faces this letdown in the year or so after high school is to celebrate the loss through meaningful mourning. Parents can help their older adolescents describe all the good things about high school that they now miss, treating those good times as grounds for confidence. Instead of just mourning the loss, they can value all the good they received. Your message is: "If you did well for yourself in high school, that just shows you have what it takes to do well for yourself again. But you must accept what is true for the majority of us. Because the world after graduation is so much larger than high school, most of us never make as big a social or performance mark for ourselves again as we thought we did then. But that doesn't mean you can't do well for yourself and make yourself happy. It only means that the world of high school is over now, and your life in the larger world has begun."

PARENTING PRESCRIPTION

1. To adjust to the change of leaving home, young people need to know that out of sight is not out of mind, that their physical and emotional place in the family is secure, and that leaving home in no way means that they are losing their home.

2. Explain to your son or daughter the financial adjustment you went through when you were starting out to show what he or she must now work through, too: at first doing without, living on a lot less money, struggling to manage, learning to get by, gradually making it, and finding some financial stability.

3. Treat homesickness empathetically for the hard social and emotional separation that it is, honor the family caring it represents, and understand that the best treatment for homesickness is adequate communication with those at home.

4. Help students who had a peak high school experience understand that, although they might never make as big a mark on the world as they seemed to make in high school, great opportunities and happiness do lie ahead, after the hardship of letting go of the old glory days with high school friends.

CHAPTER FOUR

CHALLENGE #2: MANAGING INCREASED FREEDOM

"It's a lot to deal with all at once, all that freedom. On the one hand, it was so exciting—acting like rules didn't matter. That's how I got into a lot of trouble! I never thought that ignoring parking tickets could lead to a warrant for my arrest! On the other hand, all that freedom was exhausting. More choices than I knew what to do with and no one to look over my shoulder or check up on me. I think so much freedom can be too much of a good thing. I know it sounds crazy, but sometimes I wished for some rules to go by and somebody to make them stick. Freedom turned out to be a big letdown. That's when I started thinking about joining the military or going back home. I chose home."

During trial independence, freedom can be extremely challenging for a young person. Being more on their own, last-stage adolescents discover the nature of this new freedom—a world in which there are many more decisions to make than ever before. A lot of management choices that their parents previously took care of—like paying bills, scheduling enough sleep, managing minor medical issues—are suddenly up to them. Gone are the household services, parental supervision, and family rules that took care of so many decisions affecting their life before. As one young person confessed, "There's so much more to think about now! It's exhausting!"

This is true. It's a lot to organize, to keep track of, to take care of, to accomplish, and to watch out for. What I often see in counseling last-stage adolescents is what I have come to call *decision fatigue*. These young people are simply worn out by all that they have to think about and choose to do or not to do. No longer sheltered by parents and home, they are deluged with more choices than they ever have had before. They feel overwhelmed by alternatives and obligations, invitations and opportunities, and are confused about how to prioritize them all.

And this is how it should be. The hard reality is that it takes a lot more energy to function as an independent adult than as a dependent adolescent. This is why trial independence is the period during which young people get in training, in condition, to shoulder the wearying scope of grown-up responsibility. But without the right guidance, this training can become overwhelming, and young people can boomerang back home.

There are three psychological challenges to managing all this newfound freedom:

1. Freedom and consequences
2. Freedom and self-discipline

3. Freedom and authority

Let's examine each one and how you can help guide your child through each challenge.

FREEDOM AND CONSEQUENCES

The first thing older adolescents discover during trial independence is that the freedom they desired so much isn't actually free. It comes with a powerful string attached—responsibility.

Younger adolescents often say they wanted independence, when what they really meant was social freedom—freedom from adult direction and restraint. And when they did think about social freedom, it was usually as the freedom of choice to act as they wished, which of course is only half of social freedom. The other half—the string attached, if you will—is coping with the consequence of every choice: enjoying beneficial consequences when the choice is good and confronting unhappy consequences when the choice is bad. The second half of social freedom is responsibility. *Because freedom of choice is always chained to consequence, the freedom to make one's own decisions is never free.*

One way to think about the job of parenting adolescents is the process of continually teaching the choice-consequence connection. This is important for two reasons. First, the young person learns what kind of decisions can cause what kind of outcomes (unprotected sex, for example, can lead to sexual disease or unwanted pregnancy). Second, by owning and coping with the consequences of a decision, the young person learns responsibility (she parked illegally, got a ticket, and spends her hard-earned money to pay the fine).

However, this instruction is not as easy to deliver as it seems. Sometimes we don't want to allow our teenagers to experience the consequences. And sometimes teenagers don't want to acknowledge that choices lead to consequences at all.

I recall a young person who got involved in shoplifting—not to get anything he particularly wanted but to see what he could get away with. When he got caught with the goods, his parents had the charges legally dissolved so he did not receive the consequence they feared—a juvenile record for theft. Talk to the parents, and they had good reasons for saving their son from this social consequence. "He's really a good kid, he says he's learned his lesson, and an active record could hurt his opportunities down the line." But the young man felt blameless for the entire episode. "If they wouldn't have caught me, none of this trouble would have happened. Besides, it's a stupid rule. The store's not going to miss a couple of CDs." So the lesson the young man carried forward into the last stage of his adolescence was this: "Rules are made for other people, not for me. If I get into trouble, my parents will get me out. They've done it before."

Young people who enter trial independence having been protected from the earlier errors of their ways by well-meaning parents usually have to learn lessons of responsibility from hard social reality. Once young people are out in the world, it is no time for well-meaning parents to rescue their children from facing the consequences of their ill-advised choices. Writing bad checks, not paying credit card bills, and ignoring traffic fines are common ways that young people in the trial independence stage sometimes treat their exhilarating sense of freedom. Without a parent to rescue them, last-stage adolescents discover that when they run up credit card balances, interest rates just increase what they owe. And if they cease making payments, and act as though debt will go away if they ignore it, collection agencies rudely awaken them to the obligation they have incurred.

Unwanted consequences can help educate about making choices, if parents acknowledge these consequences and allow them to bite. Because so much education during adolescence occurs after a mistake or misdeed, experiencing the outcomes of these actions can have a hugely powerful instructional effect.

Consider the young man who experiments with more dangerous substance use when he is out on his own. Promised a "great trip" by his buddies, he has a harrowing experience with hallucinogens. In this case, the bad consequence teaches a good lesson. "I'll never drop acid again!" he resolves, and he means it.

Thus, instead of rescuing children from consequences, parents should help them learn to think about the consequences beforehand. For young people, the secret to managing more freedom is taking the time to think before they act. And I'm not talking about a lot of time—just time enough for young people to take what I call the *three-question test*. They can ask themselves and answer these three questions in a matter of seconds, and their answers can save them from a lot of grief:

1. "Why would I want to do this?"
2. "What harm might it cause?"
3. "Is it worth the risk?"

Parents can advise: "If your companions won't give you the fraction of time required to think and take the three-question test, you can be pretty sure that you are facing a bad choice."

"Accidents" are another problem that arises when young people deny responsibility by claiming, "It couldn't be helped," "It wasn't my fault," "It was bad luck," or "It was an *accident*." Accidents, which are unwanted occurrences that are not considered or foreseen, are part of adolescence, because with more freedom comes greater risk of mishaps. For example, drive a car; and you risk collisions; have sex; and you risk sexual disease or pregnancy; or have a credit card; and you risk overspending.

Come trial independence, when capacity for responsibility is the only real protection a young person has against the risks of freedom, the parenting guideline needs to be that pleading "accident" is not acceptable. Some of the common pleas you'll encounter are the following:

- "I didn't mean to!" (when something important is lost)
- "I didn't know!" (when a law is broken)
- "It just happened!" (when there's a bad drug reaction)
- "There was nothing I could do!" (when two cars collide)
- "I was just unlucky!" (when only he or she was caught)

Such statements make it seem like accidents occur when adolescents are victimized by an unintended, unexpected, unpredictable, uncontrollable, or unfortunate occurrence. And in one way, this is true. In another way, it's not. The concept of accident, particularly during adolescence, is a tricky one. It's true that an accident is an unanticipated, usually unwanted, event. However, no accident ever really happens accidentally, because there is always cause for consequences that the teenager did not foresee.

The problem with accidents is not only the damage they can do but also the tendency of young people to disown responsibility by blaming them on bad breaks, other people, faulty workings, or a host of external agents and conditions. In doing so, they cast off their own complicity in what occurred. It's true, for example, that after the party, the young couple didn't intend to become pregnant, and they placed blame on the defective contraceptive they clumsily used. But they did choose to have sex.

Labeling an event as "accidental" can be a way of escaping one's share of the responsibility. After all, if young people gave more thought to their choices, better control their impulses, exercise more care, consult their foresight, they might avert many such accidents.

In any case, come adolescence, more accidents of one kind or another will happen. So, how parents should deal with accidents is the question. The answer is that if the returning adolescent, by way of excuse, claims, "It was an accident," then parents can sometimes agree and say, "Yes, we believe it was."

Then they can go on to explain what an accident really is—an unwanted outcome of some identifiable causes that surprisingly came to pass:

> *"Of course we know that you were not planning for this accident to happen, but being in the wrong place at the wrong time for your own reasons was a function of what you decided to do. And where there is choice, there is always a measure of responsibility. Let's talk about your share of responsibility so that by owning it you are less likely to have this accident again."*

There are no accidents. There is a cause for everything. That's how events occur.

For parents, during the last stage of adolescent growth, there is another guideline worth mentioning. Although bad consequences can discourage young people from making bad choices, good consequences can encourage them to make good choices. So the question for parents during this crucial training period for adult independence is, "Do you regularly give affirmation of and appreciation for all the good choices your last-stage adolescent makes?" If not, you're missing a good bet. Many times, discouraged last-stage adolescents who feel that they are "totally failing to catch hold" can benefit from the parental perspective that identifies those independent challenges that they are managing well. For example:

> *"It's true that by partying and not going to class you did fail out, but there is some good on the positive side of the ledger. You were*

able to leave and live away from home. You were able to make friends in a strange place. You were able to get and hold a part-time job to make your spending money. And you've learned some very good ways not to 'do' college if that opportunity arises again."

Then there is this hard reality to remember: Although all choices have consequences, good choices never guarantee that good consequences will follow. Freedom to go for what you want doesn't necessarily extend to the freedom to get what you want. For example, a young woman did all the work and studied very hard to go to college but didn't get into her first-choice school. Despite all her good decisions, the desired consequence did not occur. Yet disappointment aside, she gained some benefit. The consequence she sought was a goal, and the conscientious effort in pursuit of that objective just made the adolescent's determination stronger. During counseling, she makes a wonderfully healthy response: "I'll just pick the next-best college I want to attend and apply for that!" A positive outlook can create world of opportunity.

The main lesson is that it takes anticipating and learning from consequences to successfully manage freedom during trial independence. And it takes something more: self-discipline.

FREEDOM AND SELF-DISCIPLINE

Think of the challenge of self-discipline this way. Self-discipline is the willpower to make yourself do what is good for you when it doesn't necessarily feel good to do it. Or, self-discipline is the willpower to keep yourself from doing what is bad for you when temptation makes it hard to refuse.

Come the onset of adolescence (around age 9–13), young people break the boundaries of childhood to create more room to grow, because they don't want to be defined and treated as "just a child" anymore. The room to grow opens up an enormous amount of choice, some of it resistant and some of it exploratory.

At this stage, young people have grown out of the *age of command* and into the *age of consent.* In childhood, they thought that parents had the authority to dictate what they must and must not do, but now they realize that parents can't make them do things or stop them without their cooperation. It's an exhilarating feeling for an adolescent to know that even though setting conditions and constraints is up to his or her parents, the most powerful people in his or her life, freedom of choice is now in his or her own hands.

The age of consent, however, brings a sobering realization, as well. Young people have to manage much more freedom than they know what to do with, more than they can comfortably manage. This is partly because they lack the capacity to constructively structure all this freedom. Knowing this, they give their parents their consent to partly "run" their lives, to help keep them organized and on track. From here on, parents do not strive for control (which they never really had); they work for consent—to get their child to agree to go along with what the parents want and believe is best.

So, for example, although a daughter might complain about and protest parental discipline, she also accepts the necessity of it, of doing what parents want when she knows she doesn't have to. After all, she lives in a family, not a prison. "All right, I'll stay home, but I won't forgive you for not letting me go!" She resents her parents for providing the order that she knows she needs and still depends on, but is not yet mature enough to provide for herself. This is why parenting during adolescence is often a thankless proposition.

The most long-lasting contribution parents can make with their discipline is to teach their children to internalize it as self-discipline. *The greater purpose of parental discipline is to teach the adolescent sufficient self-discipline to responsibly govern his or her life.* Developing self-discipline is how the adolescent keeps his or her increased freedom of choice within constructive limits. Those young people who enter trial independence with insufficient self-discipline are more likely to come home after freedom has gotten the better of them and they have fared for the worse.

When young people's self-discipline breaks down, it usually happens in one or more of these six ways:

1. *Organization*—They have insufficient power to keep themselves *organized,* and so they forget important commitments and obligations, such as when college class assignments are due: "I can't keep track of it all!"

2. *Direction*—They can't set a future *direction* and so lack the capacity to plan goals or objectives. For example, they might flounder out of one dead-end job and into another: "I'm not getting anywhere!"

3. *Motivation*—They can't maintain *motivation* and so can't sustain their efforts to try. For example, resolutions they make to control spending don't last: "Sooner or later I just give up!"

4. *Instruction*—They can't turn failure or mistakes into positive *instruction* for themselves. For example, they keep drinking too much and getting into difficulty but don't connect drunken choices with troubling consequences: "I don't know why it happened again!"

5. *Supervision*—They can't subject their behavior to adequate *supervision*. For example, they can't consistently monitor their conduct on the job to maintain adequate performance: "I can't be expected to examine everything I do!"

6. *Correction*—They can't modify misbehavior with *correction*. For example, they refuse to alter the errors of their ways with their roommates because it feels unfair to do so: "Why should I have to be the one to change?"

It is only by managing to become self-organized, self-directive, self-instructive, self-supervising, self-motivating, and self-corrective that older adolescents will be able to claim successful independence as self-disciplined, freestanding adults.

Thus, when parents see a breakdown in self-discipline as responsible for their son's or daughter's return home, they can help their child identify some parts of this essential skill that they need to work on. They can suggest how their child can constructively pay attention to becoming better organized, directed, motivated, instructed, supervised, or corrected, and they can ask whether they can help mentor their child in doing so. They can describe, for example, techniques for organizing personal and job life that have proved useful to them. Learning specific techniques that parents have developed to discipline their own lives can be powerfully instructive.

An obvious opportunity for young people to learn some self-discipline while still growing up with their family (and one that becomes extremely important in college) is homework. Doing homework is usually not how teenagers want to spend their free time. But the primary value of homework is that consistently managing one's studies in high school teaches a work ethic; doing homework helps develop the self-discipline to do work. Young people who develop a work ethic will have the benefit of that self-discipline when they are on their own.

Other common sources of self-discipline are training for sports, holding a job, and saving money. In sports, trying to keep up with and do better than the competition can teach a work ethic through dedication to practice, conditioning, and playing hard. Holding a part-time or summer job in high school teaches one to commit to work, even when it doesn't always feel congenial to go. And saving money teaches one to deny temptation and delay gratification to meet some future goal or objective.

In their own adulthood, parents have internalized self-discipline as part of the necessary labor of daily life. For growing adolescents, however, this self-mastery can be hard to learn. Consider homework again. In many cases, high school adolescents may still have to depend on the supervision of their parents for discipline to get homework done, through their parents' reminders and checking in until it is accomplished. By junior year, however, parents may want to turn the matter of homework over to their children and let them struggle to impose this self-discipline on themselves. So, to a college-bound adolescent in high school, I've heard parents say something like this: "How consistently you do homework shapes the study habits you will take to college. From here on, maintaining that consistency is no longer an issue between you and us; it is up to you. It is now a matter between you and the self-discipline you will need to responsibly manage your future studies when you are more on your own."

For many young people, treating senior year as a time to take easy classes, let down academic effort, and party hard with friends for a long goodbye can undercut the self-discipline needed when starting college. In effect, they enter freshman year out of training, and it can cost them. Young people don't understand that the work ethic, or lack of it, practiced near the end of high school is the work habit that they will take to college or into their work life. Self-discipline is the mainstay of a successful trial independence. It takes self-discipline, for example, for college students to get themselves up to go to class, to do assignments, and to turn them in on time. It is easier to sleep in, put off assignments, and turn them in late or not at all. It also takes self-discipline at a party with friends to keep one drink from leading to another and then to drunkenness.

At a time when many of one's peers are out having a good time, though, self-discipline may not seem like much fun. It does, however, offer lasting rewards. When young people set themselves a task or make a resolution, mobilize determination, assert self-control, apply effort, and successfully meet the challenge, they build self-esteem for having accomplished what felt very hard to do. Now, they feel empowered for having achieved their goal and for doing it on their own. And in the process, through practice, they have further strengthened the willpower or work ethic on which self-discipline depends.

Two reasonably common life decisions that arise at this age in response to feeling that self-discipline is lacking are to take a gap year to develop the self-discipline necessary for college, or to join the military in search of the self-discipline that regimented life has to teach. If a young person wants to take a gap year, agree on conditions that he or she will be responsible for providing a significant amount of self-support. This way, the self-discipline of holding a job and paying at least part of his or her expenses will create a more grown-up experience. As for joining the military to lead a more disciplined life, help the young person evaluate the serious time commitment and risks involved. Whether coming from family or (less commonly) from military life, external discipline must become internalized for self-discipline to grow. Now the young person must become his or her own authority. This last part, though, can be very hard to do.

FREEDOM AND AUTHORITY

For the last-stage adolescent, two aspects of authority can be problematic—*external authority* and *internal authority.*

Be it external or internal, authority limits freedom by making demands and by imposing restraints. In situations of external authority, the problem adolescents frequently encounter is that they, feeling more grown-up now, are less tolerant of adult authority, such as a manager at work, an instructor at college, or a police officer on the street. In the words of one young man, "The more grown up I get, the less I like being told what to do." For some young people, trial independence is a time when they tolerate external adult authority less than ever before.

Case in point: consider the very personable twenty-two-year-old who interviews well and has no trouble getting jobs. The problem is that he has a terrible time holding them down. He feels too independent for a manager to order him around, so he argues back, and he doesn't like bending his life to a work schedule, so he often arrives late. The combination of both of his issues with authority has contributed to his losing many jobs. He rebels against external authority, at his own cost.

Then, of course, there are the battles of a young person who feels like this is a time to play by his or her set of rules and not the ones that society sets. For example, a young woman who preferred to spend her rent money on more immediate pleasures for several months comes back to her apartment only to find it locked against her, with all her belongings unavailable inside. "I guess I didn't think the rent terms were that serious," she says. Sometimes it takes the enforcement of the consequences of such violations to teach what no amount of warning can convince.

Trial independence is also a stage during which a lot of law-breaking can occur. It's like the limit testing that goes on early adolescence to see which adult rules are real, but now there are more serious consequences. Young people (particularly under the influence of substances) can be charged with, for example, assault, public disorder, and selling drugs. With respect to money, they can be arrested for nonpayment of fines, writing bad checks, charging things on other people's credit cards, shoplifting, and pawning what does not belong to them. Some charm artists who are very smart, good with words, and likable can talk their way out of a lot, but not forever. For parents, if their son or daughter gets caught in some kind of lawbreaking during trial independence, it is usually best to let the young person deal with the weight of the consequences to discourage his or her bid for illicit freedom from happening again. From here on out society will treat them as adults, not juveniles.

To move from battling *external authority* to compliance, young people must learn to work with the social powers that be. This means following the rules and requirements that social institutions set. Learning to respect and work with *internal authority* requires learning to work with the personal power within. It requires establishing one's own rule-making authority (which is partly reflective of external authority), telling yourself what you must and may not do, and obeying your own personal commands. Some extremely rebellious older adolescents actually rebel against their own authority, refusing to do what they have told themselves to do or not to do. For example, there was the young woman who kept sneaking into the kitchen in the middle of the night to steal her roommate's groceries. "I know I shouldn't take my roommate's food, but I'm hungry so why shouldn't I?" Or there was the angry young man in counseling who declared: "I refuse to be ordered around, even by me!" It took working through some hard consequences for him to learn to work with and not against himself.

In trial independence, young people have to socialize themselves to follow so many of society's rules. For example, yes, you have to show up at work on time if you are to keep the job. Yes, you have to pay for electricity on time if you want to keep the lights on and the TV running. Yes, you have to pay your rent if you want a place to stay. Yes, you have to pay for traffic violations to avoid worse consequences if you don't. By taking on the authority for these decisions, young people come closer to responsibly handling the freedoms that independence brings.

PARENTING PRESCRIPTION

1. Help your adolescent understand that freedom isn't free, because a choice always leads to a consequence, and when a consequence is troublesome, he or she must manage it by assuming some responsibility for dealing with that trouble.

2. Support your child by strengthening his or her powers of organization, direction, instruction, supervision, motivation, and correction, which build self-discipline.

3. Help your child identify the self-defeating costs of rebelling against legitimate social authority, or against his or her own internal authority, to preserve personal freedom.

CHAPTER FIVE

CHALLENGE #3: FLUNKING OUT OF COLLEGE

"Here's what I found out about college. It's just four more years of high school all over again. Go to class, listen to teachers, write notes, get homework, take tests, and do papers. Except now no one keeps after you; you're on your own. You're away from home, and most of your college friends are out having a good time, so it's really hard to get your school-work done. It can snowball on you. Stay up late, sleep in, miss a class, get behind, and you begin a downhill slide. Then you promise yourself to study more tomorrow night, but you end up hanging out or partying instead. Pretty soon you've lost too much ground to catch up. It wasn't the work that was hard to do but getting myself to do the work. Then telling my parents that I'd flunked out and wasted a lot of their money. Now I'm back home to get myself organized. They gave me six months and then I have to be out on my own. I wish I'd taken care of business at college."

According to *The Journal of College Student Retention*, "only about 66% of high school graduates attend college and about 50% of those who attend college earn a bachelor's degree." Obviously, this low percentage of college completion varies from institution to institution. Those where admission is most competitive tend to get the more qualified and committed students and hence have higher retention rates.

Major reasons students drop out of college include financial hardship, outside obligations to a full-time job or to family, social alienation, and inadequate academic and psychological preparation. Sometimes, financially, they or their parents simply cannot afford to pay the continuing expense. In terms of outside obligations, full-time work and/or family commitments leave insufficient time and energy for study. Academically, students might not have gained adequate skills, knowledge, or preparation in high school to successfully accomplish college-level work. Socially, they might feel marginalized or isolated and unable to find a comfortable way to fit in. Psychologically, they might lack sufficient maturity or self-management skills to make the consistent commitment to class attendance and study that maintaining a good academic standing requires.

It is the psychological factor that I believe is the greatest contributor to last-stage adolescents' flunking out, and the one this chapter is primarily about. Quite simply, many of today's late-stage adolescents do not enter college prepared to successfully cope with the demands of college life.

There are three challenges that make finding and holding one's footing in college hard to accomplish:

1. The problem of being a student
2. The problem of commitment
3. The problem of readiness

In this chapter, we will explore each of these challenges, as well as how you can help your child through them if, or before, he or she flunks out of school.

THE PROBLEM OF BEING A STUDENT

A young woman once said to me: "When people—adults, I mean—ask me what I'm doing and I tell them that I'm a college student, I say it like I'm apologizing, which in a way I am."

"Why is that?" I asked. "What do you have to apologize for?"

She gave me her demeaning definition of being a student. "A college student is just a person in preparation—someone who's getting ready to do something but hasn't done anything yet. As a student, I have no socially useful definition. I'm just in training for adulthood. Until I graduate and start contributing, I don't count for much." She treated the label of "student" as an admission that she lacked worthwhile standing, and many students do this.

In addition, the authority of professors can cause intimidation for students. A student's role in the class is a submissive one—to listen to what the professor has to say and to comply with the professor's conditions and demands. For a young person who is at the age of wanting to be his or her own authority, it is easy for them to feel diminished by this need for deference and compliance. It can take a lot of courage and confidence to speak up, to question, to disagree when there is something they want to say. How timidly or boldly one interacts in class has much to do with how negatively or positively one deems the student role.

The only good solution to the problem of the "unapproachable" authority figure of the professor is for students to dare to approach the professor and engage him or her in conversation about whatever they need or is of concern to them. Years ago I heard a father give this advice to his departing son. "When you get to college, there are three things I want you to remember. First, even though you work for those professors, they are paid by us to work their best for you, so go to all their classes to get the best they have to offer. Second, to take charge of your education, you need to ask them whatever it is you need or want to know. They are in charge of what they teach you, but you are responsible for asking questions to make sure you are being effectively taught. And third, professors are just people, and you should make enough effort to get to know them so that they get to know you." Speaking up to college professors reduces the intimidating power of their authority.

Over the years, I've heard variations on the demeaning "I'm just a student" response, all tending in the same direction: that the designation "student" often doesn't generate much self-respect. Because the student designation is one of dependence, compliance, preparation, low status, and few real-world responsibilities, it can be hard on one's self-esteem.

Four strategies can help prevent college students' erosion of self-esteem:

1. Choosing a college major that is directed toward an occupational objective, like becoming a teacher, for example, helps one feel that college preparation has some applied value, which gives a sense of purpose to being a student.

2. Volunteering out in the community can broaden experience and deepen understanding of the real world while providing a role identity that goes beyond being just a "student." Young people will be valued for their contributions and will be identified as helpers and service providers.

3. Obtaining an internship, even an unpaid one, can place one in an occupational setting that confers a definition and standing that classroom education cannot. Functioning in an employment setting similar to what one will seek after graduation provides on-the-job training that marks the value of one's education.

4. Often most powerful is holding a part-time job, an activity that generally boosts psychological independence and can make graduation more likely.

When I mention this last idea, part-time work, many parents often balk. Even parents who rely on student loan support resist the idea. "Part-time work will only place more demands upon him and will take time away from his studies," they argue. But I dis-agree. The job demands will be supportive, and students already devote time away from their studies to pursue other nonacademic (recreational) interests.

It is very hard for many last-stage adolescents to grow up in college because they are treated as dependent in two ways that promote immaturity. When they are totally defined by the student role, young people are treated as dependents in preparation for adulthood. When they are totally financed by their parents, they are treated as dependents to be supported until adulthood. On both counts, growing up to achieve more responsibility and inde-pendence can be delayed.

What a part-time job can offer is a more adult definition in the workplace and some sense of financial independence, from generating one's own income. This is why there can be a world of difference between the employed and the unemployed student. The real-world experience of necessary part-time employment helps a last-stage adolescent grow up in ways that a fully subsidized world of college study usually cannot. Simply put, students who work part-time to help pay their way through college often tend to be more invested in pursuing and completing their education. By earning part of their way in life, they take more responsibility for their life. In partly supporting themselves, they earn respect for themselves as providers.

Parents who decide to have their children go the part-time job route in college simply need to make clear in advance the basic expenses that they are committed to underwriting and the discretionary ones that will be their child's responsibility to assume. Then parents and student can try to estimate what those yearly expenses will amount to so that the student can get a sense of how much he or she must earn. I've seen some young people bank their summer and Christmas break jobs to reach their goal of not needing a part-time job during the academic year. In most cases, though, working students simply get a part-time job, maybe fifteen or twenty hours a week, and earn their expenses as they go, and as they grow.

As I've counseled working college students over the years, it has struck me how the distraction of having a part-time job can concentrate a student in a number of ways on taking care of academic business at college. Here are just a few of the ways I have observed:

- Affirming that they have some knowledge, skill, or service to provide that the world of work deems worth paying for
- Providing them with a grown-up work role in addition to a growing-up student role
- Creating adult, real-world responsibility for them to meet
- Strengthening their work ethic with respect to doing what they don't always want to do
- Enabling them to earn some independent income
- Giving them some pride and self-satisfaction from supporting themselves financially
- Requiring discipline to meet a schedule (skip a class and you miss a lecture, but skip a shift and you lose a job)

- Providing them with grown-up experience working for a boss, getting along with co-workers, and serving the buying public
- Making them more mindful of how they manage money now that they are working hard to earn it
- Showing them how little they will make at an entry-level job, which causes them to place more value on achieving a college education
- Building their employment history for future jobs
- Making it easier to honor a class schedule now that they are keeping a work schedule
- Feeling productive because they get some immediate material benefit from their efforts that studying alone cannot provide
- Keeping them busy enough working and studying so it's harder to afford as much play and party time as their non-working student friends
- Giving them some financial stake in the education they are receiving
- Making them more serious about finishing their college education so they can finally get a "real" job

In general, it's very hard for many last-stage adolescents to grow up enough in college to be able to finish college, unless they have some significant demands for independence while they are doing their studies, too. This is where a part-time job can help to broaden their sense of what it means to be a student. A part-time job is not a magic bullet or a guarantee for graduation, but it often can provide some help when it comes to preventing flunking out. And those students who held part-time jobs in high school tend to be even more inclined to continue to do so in college.

Another problem to consider is this one, encountered by a recent college graduate who had no employment history at all. When it came time for job applications, he had no evidence of previous employability to bring to the table. According to him, the interviewer was nonplussed by his college credential. "The guy just looked at my application and then at me and asked me how come I'd never held a job? Was there some problem about not getting along with people? Couldn't I hack an eight-to-five schedule week in and week out? Was there a lack of motivation? He told me going to class and going to work were not the same, that good grades were not evidence of good work habits. How come I had no job references to support my application? No history of service, retail, clerical, sales, or manual labor? He said I needed more work experience before applying there." In this case, a college degree did provide the young man some educational preparation, but that was no substitute for work experience.

This example does bear on those students who do *not* flunk out but often pay the price of only having been a student and nothing else. Come graduation, their long education as a student finally comes to an end. Unless they have significant employment history, they have spent virtually their whole lives in a state of educational preparation. When college ends, the sheltered role of student falls away and they feel stripped of definition, motivation, confidence, and purpose as they face a large, impersonal world in which they are expected to make their way.

For a while, they can feel stunned and discouraged and overwhelmed. They don't know what to do with themselves; they don't know whether the world has any place of gainful employment for them. Because there is nobody telling them what to do, they must direct themselves. So even these "successful" college graduates may find themselves moving back home to live rent-free, to look for work, to control their expenses, to start to pay off what they owe, and to plan for independent living that will not happen right away.

THE PROBLEM OF COMMITMENT

Another psychological problem that many students encounter is the problem of commitment. It takes educational commitment to complete college, and many students are deficient in this regard. Quite simply, they have other motivations in mind when they attend college. For example, going to college can be more of a default decision—it can defer answering the question "What else could I be doing with my life?" Or it can be a way to delay independence and put life in the real world on hold: "I can buy some more time." Or it can feel obligatory: "I'm expected to go, because this was always my parents' plan." Or it can feel essential for employability, since many young people believe that, without a college degree, they can't make their way in the world: "I need a college degree to get a job." Or they can go for the fun of it, so that college becomes not a means to an end but the end—a good time—in itself: "College is for freedom away from home."

They hope that college will be different—more interesting and exciting and motivating—than high school. But college turns out to be four or five more years of typical schooling, just like the twelve years of compulsory education they already know. It's the same schedule of classes, lectures, papers, tests, and projects, all assigned by adults, who continue to tell them what to do and grade them on their instructional compliance. Many students enter college significantly burned out on formal education, and they are not really ready to commit to more. And while they were in high school, they had the support of having to go to class; at college, there is no one to make them go except themselves.

To give college teachers their due, their instructional job becomes very difficult when young people enter class unprepared, uncommitted, undisciplined, and even feeling entitled. The *entitlement* seems to come from the sense that in college, unlike high school, they are customers; they are in college to be served. Therefore, they should not have to work too hard, at least not as hard as they did to get in. As such, they expect that the teachers should make the material easy and interesting to learn, not too demanding, and definitely not boring. The notion that students must independently bring their interests to the table can be difficult for some young people to accept. So, in the words of one disenchanted young man: "I skipped classes because none of the teachers at college could motivate me." Thus the buck of assuming educational responsibility for himself was passed.

The students who treat college as a period of deferred responsibility find it a hard place to grow up. "College is a good place to hide," was how one young man put it. "You don't really do much of anything except the minimum to pass. Nobody knows how productive you are with your time except you, and you're not telling. College is a great cover, a great place to look serious and have fun." For this student, it's obvious why flunking out was so traumatic. All of a sudden, he lost his student standing, his financial support, and his invisibility, and he was now expected to be accountable, to find work, and to do something with his life. In his words: "I've lost my excuse for being unemployed. I'm not free to drift anymore."

So, if you sense that "drifting" has caused your child's flunking out and return home, and if you believe that this attitude may still be in play in his or her desire to try college again, you might want to set your child on a more serious course of strengthened commitment. You might want to let your child know that you will finance college on a yearly basis going forward, that continuing educational support is contingent on a full-faith effort to successfully take and complete a full academic load. You might also want to limit the number of years of college that you will finance—if your child needs more courses after that point to finish, it is his or her responsibility to pay. This includes the additional course requirements that result from changing majors multiple times.

Sometimes the issue of commitment isn't just about flunking out, though. Sometimes at college, young people take a full course load to qualify for student status; but then course failures, incompletes, or drops slow their academic progress. Then they sign up for another semester to justify continuing parental support, which the parents, in good faith, agree to provide. In such cases, it usually works best for parents to take two actions to encourage the growth of commitment. First, they should let their son or daughter know that nonbasic living expenses, like rent, cell phone, and cable costs, will be his or hers to cover. Second, parents should keep offering their support for education, but on a different basis. For example: "We will continue to pay for your classes, but instead of paying for them at the start, we will pay on the back end. You earn enough to front the money for any classes you want to take, and we will reimburse you for all the classes you successfully complete." If the student wants to commit to his or her college education, he or she will accept the offer.

Finally, ask this commitment question: Is the student personally committed to college, or is he or she just attending because the parents are committed to the idea of college? With the statement "I'm here because my parents are making me go," the student disowns personal responsibility. That reasoning, of course, is psychologically flawed, because parents can't force their college-age child to do anything. Moreover, since the outset of adolescence, the young person has known that parental commands have no power unless they are coupled with the child's consent.

In this way, college attendance becomes a conflicted decision with a self-defeating outcome when the young person rebels against self-interest to spite his or parents, affirming the old proverb "You can lead a horse to water, but you cannot make him drink." Notice that the rebellion is usually not against going to college, which the adolescent likely deems a worthy objective, but against his parents for forcing the issue. To this adolescent, the issue worth fighting for is this: Who is going to be in charge of my life?

So the result is this immature, my-parents-are-making-me compromise. The young person actively complies with what parents want by attending college but passively resists what parents want by refusing to do satisfactory work. The outcome is that the student wins by losing and loses by winning. What about winning by winning?

The antidote to rebellion is challenge. Instead of *dependently* defining oneself against authority for opposition's sake, the young person can self-define *independently* by embracing the challenge of college on his or her own behalf: "I got here because my parents wanted me to get here, but what I accomplish here is not for them but for my satisfaction, my benefit, my betterment, my life, and my future." On the path of rebellion, the young person casts off responsibility by focusing on opposing what he or she is being told to do. On the path of challenge, the young person embraces responsibility by independently choosing to lead his or her own life on his her own behalf. Acting dependently at an age that requires more independence is self-defeating.

So how do you help your rebelling child see this path? Perhaps you could say this: "We are not in the business of controlling your life, but we are in the business of giving you an opportunity in life. What you make of that opportunity is up to you. If you can't go to college partly for us (because we believe it is in your best long-term interests) and then work at college entirely for you, then it's probably not worth our expense or your time."

With the right approach and strategies, you can help you child understand his or her commitment issues and move past them to achieve success. Keep in mind, though, that although commitment is normally the main reason for this behavior, sometimes it is actually due to fear of the future (see Chapter 13.) In that case, young people are simply scared of the prospect of journeying into an unknown future with no clear path and no guaranteed outcomes, and of having to make all those important decisions on their own. Rebellion against their own self-interest slows down the prospect of the future's arrival. Factor in this possibility as you mentor your child through trial independence.

THE PROBLEM OF READINESS

As mentioned earlier, the figures are pretty dramatic: on average, about 50 percent or more of entering students fail to graduate from the college in which they first enroll, if they graduate at all. What's the matter with these institutions and students, anyway? Is higher education failing to adequately engage students, or are students failing to make an adequate effort? The answer is, both are usually true.

The problem is that higher education assumes that last-stage adolescent students are ready to act grown-up, whereas students assume that high school study habits are adequate for college. Both assumptions are wrong, and this is something that should change.

Expectations on both sides need to be clarified and reconciled: *a college student is still an adolescent, and college is not the same as high school.*

It takes a certain amount of *psychological independence* to complete college. Young people who are psychologically independent take care of business by keeping their completion, commitment, and consistency skills in good working order.

- In terms of *completion*, they finish what they start.
- In terms of *commitment*, they keep their promises to themselves and others.
- In terms of *consistency*, they maintain continuity of healthy or productive effort.

Young people who cannot carry through with their good intentions can fall prey to three kinds of *psychological dependence*:

- *Lack of completion*—They can start a lot of well-intended projects, but they can't finish much: "I meant to get it done, but I didn't."
- *Lack of commitment*—They can make all kinds of promises to themselves and others, but they can't make good on many of them: "I have a hard time keeping my word."
- *Lack of consistency*—They can work for their best interests in spurts, but they can't maintain continuity of effort over the long haul: "Sooner or later I start slacking off."

Young people who get mired in these acts of psychological dependence injure their self-esteem, lower their self-confidence, and reduce their motivation. In the words of one young man, "I keep spinning my wheels and finally give up because I'm not getting anywhere." When students get into a habit of not doing, nothing gets done. This is what can happen when young people let their self-discipline slide in their last year in high school for the sake of having fun. As one ex-college freshman explained: "When I slacked off senior year in high school, I didn't realize how the loss of study habits would work against me later. When I got to college, I couldn't gear my will to work back up."

I think the young man was correct. When nothing gets done for long enough, the accumulated work becomes overwhelming, which is when a lot of students drop out or flunk out. Because of their intermittent effort, they do end up "spinning their wheels." They can't seem to get traction. They can't seem to get anywhere.

Adolescents facing these issues have a difficult time readying themselves for college coursework. And last-stage adolescents make up most of the student body that higher education is challenged to teach. A challenge it is: frustrated teachers wonder, "Why don't students stay enrolled, speak up to teachers, turn work in on time, and show up regularly to class?" The answer is because young people have conflicts with four kinds of responsibilities that support true independence:

1. *Meeting study commitments*—The dependent part of them rebels against their own internal authority and says, "Don't work that hard, it's easier to quit." So they drop out rather than hang in there, thus defeating their own self-interest.

2. *Speaking up to a teacher*—They have not yet assumed sufficient adult independence to assert equal worth and standing in the conversation. So they avoid talking with professors, and by not asking important questions, they fail to inform and influence the course of their own education.

3. *Turning work in on time*—They still resent having a schedule set for them. So they turn in assignments on their own time, which is late. Soon, late becomes later, and then later becomes not at all.

4. *Showing up regularly to class*—They have yet to develop sufficient self-discipline to maintain that consistency of effort independently. So they let themselves skip one day, one day leads to skipping the next, and soon they are mostly not attending class.

All these conflicts play out within the student who wants to act grown-up and also doesn't. College is where young people often wage the final battle for adolescent independence. They are fighting within themselves, for and against their own authority, to make themselves do what they don't want to do, and they are acting that resistance out against their professors. For many young people, college becomes the gateway passage from the end of adolescence into young adulthood. This passage can be a struggle not because college is so difficult (although some students were not sufficiently prepared academically in high school) but because assuming full responsibility and acting grown-up is hard to do—as it is for us all.

What can a parent do to help?

- Maintain adult demands and expect your child to meet them.
- Accept no excuses, make no exceptions, and attempt no rescues.
- Listen respectfully and empathetically.
- Do not criticize your child for not measuring up to the expectations of college.
- Encourage learning more responsibility by facing the consequences of how your child chose to act.

WHEN YOUR CHILD FLUNKS OUT

If your child has returned home after flunking out, it can initially be quite a shock. In fact, for most parents, the news of their child's flunking out comes as a surprise. In the words of one parent: "A few days ago we learned that our eighteen-year-old received mostly failing grades for her first year at college and was not invited to return. We were shocked at this news, since she reported only passing grades, and we trusted she was telling us the truth!" Then, to double up on their anger, there was the financial waste: "We sacrificed a lot for her to have a chance for college. We did our part, but she didn't do hers!"

This is quite common when a young person flunks out of college. Most young people know it's happening long before they tell their parents, and when parents do hear the news, they feel to some degree betrayed.

After they have shared their unhappiness, however, parents do need to get about the business of helping the young person move on. For example, when the guilty and regretful adolescent laments, "A whole year of college and I didn't learn anything!" parents need to disagree. "That's not true," they can honestly say. "Tell us what you did and didn't do that contributed to your flunking out."

Imagine that your child then says this:

> "I played and partied late with friends. I drank too much and smoked too much pot. I slept in and missed classes. I lied to you about what was going on. I didn't write papers or turned them in late. I didn't do the assigned reading. I watched a lot of movies. I wasted a lot of time on the Internet. I didn't study for tests. I stopped exercising and ate too much junk food. I made lots of promises to do the work and kept breaking them. And even though I slept in a lot, I was tired and stressed most of the time from not getting enough sleep."

Now, that is probably a frustrating response. But what if you answer like this:

> "See, you learned a whole lot about how not to do college. Don't play around, party late, drink and take drugs, sleep in, and miss classes. Don't lie to us about what's going on, skip papers or hand them in late, or watch a lot of movies. Don't waste time on the Internet, neglect to study for tests, stop exercising, eat too much junk food, make and break work promises to yourself, or short yourself on sleep. See what I mean? You've learned a lot! Now if you ever try college again, you'll know exactly what not to do."

This response gives young people the right perspective for moving forward in their independence, whether or not that means returning to college. In fact, for many students who flunk out and return home, doing so doesn't end their college education. They may go back to finish the education they interrupted feeling more seasoned and resolved from the hard experience of being out for a while, or they may find somewhere else to continue what they once hopefully began. Failing to engage with college the first time is no excuse not to try again after they have taken a responsible, hardworking time-out from school.

So when a young person comes home having fallen casualty to psychological dependence, parents should support the initiative and accomplishment that it takes to build up psychological independence. To this end, while children are at home, parents should expect and insist on the following:

- *Completion*: "We expect you to finish what you start."
- *Consistency*: "We expect you to maintain continuity of healthy effort."
- *Commitment*: "We expect you to keep your agreements and promises."

It is only by building up these three pillars of psychological independence that self-esteem, faith, and forward momentum can be restored. Then your child can say with confidence, "I can follow through on my goals, I can keep up what matters to me, and I can count on my word."

Finally, it is always worth raising the fundamental investment question to evaluate the expenditure of time, energy, and money involved in college: "Could I invest the next four years and thousands of dollars differently in myself to better prepare myself for an employable adulthood, rather than spending this significant amount of life time, energy, and money (all of which are non-refundable) in getting further formal education?" In some cases, parents and children might find that college was not the right path after all, and that young people are better served by directly entering the workforce.

PARENTING PRESCRIPTION

1. If your child is planning to return to college on some basis, encourage him or her to treat being a student with respect by working hard for themselves and their future, while engaging in service and internship activities that affirm a sense of social worth and occupational purpose.

2. Strengthen your child's commitment to returning to college by requiring him or her to earn and pay part of the way.

3. Address the need to develop psychological independence—capacities for successful completion, meeting commitments, and maintaining consistent work habits.

CHAPTER SIX

CHALLENGE #4: UNEMPLOYMENT

"I thought I had it made, or at least had it started. I was making all my bills and then suddenly I'm out of work. Laid off, just like that! Last hired, first fired—I learned that much. Back to reading want ads, making phone calls, doing Internet searches, filling out applications, sending out resumes, trying for interviews. But no takers. It was pretty discouraging and scary. That's when my bills started to get on top of me. My mom couldn't afford to help me out, but she would take me back in. So that's why I came home. It's easier to look for work when you're broke if you have a paid place to stay."

When older adolescents come back home after being unable to keep or find employment, as happens much more frequently when the economy goes down, they can be in a hard place, both mentally and financially. During this time, they typically will face three major psychological challenges, the three R's:

1. Recovering from job loss
2. Restoring resiliency
3. Relocating in the workforce

The challenge of recovery is to honor the loss and neither to deny it nor to dwell on the pain, which precludes moving forward. The challenge of resiliency is keeping mind, body, and attitude in positive working order to maintain motivation. The challenge of relocation is to turn up and pursue job possibilities. In each of these challenges, parents have a supportive role.

RECOVERY FROM JOB LOSS

Entering the workforce feels like an adult thing to do, and it is. Exchanging labor for money is what the adolescent will need to be doing throughout his or her adult life. And in doing so, they can develop many strengths:

- It takes *initiative* to search and find a job opening.
- It takes *assertiveness* to interview for a position.
- It takes *responsibility* to discharge the duties of a job.
- It takes *discipline* to show up for work on schedule each day.
- It takes *compliance* with authority to work for a boss.
- It takes *cooperation* with peers to get along with co-workers.
- It takes *patience* with customers to work with the public.
- It takes *maturity* about spending to live within the income made.

In addition, probably no activity empowers a sense of youthful autonomy as powerfully as having a job does. Consider five personal benefits to the young person of having a job:

- *Independence*—A job is how most people finance their independence. With a job comes the means to earn one's keep and pay one's way.
- *Identity*—A job is a significant part of one's identity. With a job comes a sense of social definition.
- *Self-worth*—A job affirms self-worth. With a job comes recognition that one has sufficient skill and knowledge to merit economic value in the marketplace.
- *Belonging*—A job provides an employment system in which one belongs. With a job comes membership among a community of fellow workers.
- *Purpose*—A job provides a sense of purpose. With a job comes a worthwhile way to pursue self-interest and to do something useful in the world.

In all five areas, a job is a kind of lifeline to survival. That's why people refer to their job as how they "make a living." And it's why losing a job can feel like a kind of death, a loss of making a living.

Psychologically, job loss can entail the loss of any of the five benefits that employment confers, or it can mask many losses in one. Depending on the individual, some of those losses will be more painful than others. Parents can help their child identify which losses are most troubling by localizing the damage. It's like when the doctor asks, "Where does it hurt?" Specify the area of injury, and you can focus on the particular need for recovery.

Consider the case of a young person who was laid off for no reason other than being the most recently hired:

- The loss of independence can cause feelings of *anger* and *anxiety* in response: "It's not fair that they let me go when I was working hard and doing well; how will I take care of myself now?"
- The loss of identity can cause feelings of *grief* and *emptiness*: "I was just building a career for myself; now it's been taken away and I've got nothing left to be!"
- The loss of self-worth can cause feelings of *inadequacy* and even *shame*: "This goes to show I can't hold a job, that something's the matter with me!"
- The loss of belonging can cause feelings of *loneliness* and *isolation*: "I have no workplace where I can go each day, where I belong."
- The loss of purpose can cause feelings of *aimlessness* and *pointlessness*: "Without my job, I have nothing constructive to do with myself."

There are ways for parents to address each of these feelings. First, parents must be sensitive to their child's initial emotional response to job loss. Then, in addition to listening and being empathetic, they can provide some needed perspective to help frame the losses with which their son or daughter is contending:

- *Loss of independence*—Parents can suggest that job loss is an event that usually happens multiple times over a person's occupational life. They can explain how job security is not guaranteed for anyone: "The good thing about this loss is that, at an early age, you have the opportunity to learn how to cope with this challenge and how to move on to your next station of employment, both of which are skills that will likely serve you well on occasion later on."

- *Loss of identity*—Parents can suggest that any time you let your job define all of who you are, you are making it matter too much. They can explain how it is important to have many aspects of life that describe, in your own mind, the person you are: "If you do this, when you lose a job, it doesn't feel like all of who you are is lost. Better for a job to be part of you, not all of you."

- *Loss of self-worth*—Parents can suggest that job termination not be taken too personally. They can explain how treating oneself as a failure when a job didn't last or work out makes a hard experience extremely punishing: "If a job doesn't fit, or even if you are fired for cause, that doesn't mean you are unfit for employment in general. Don't let the loss of a job cause you to lose faith and confidence in your employability."

- *Loss of belonging*—Parents can suggest creating community elsewhere until their child finds the next job. They can explain how jobs do provide an important community of relationships that are missed once a job is lost: "For companionship, consider joining some recreational, social, or support groups so you don't have to move through this time feeling all alone."

- *Loss of purpose*—Parents can suggest investing in other pursuits that provide a sustaining sense of direction and meaning. They can explain how continuing to work in activities and toward objectives that matter on an unpaid basis can be sustaining: "While you are looking for another job, you could also volunteer your time where it is needed; even take an unpaid internship at a job you'd like. This way, although you're out of paid employment, you'll continue to have some work to contribute and gather experience to advance yourself."

At this point, it is important to recognize that there are two types of job loss during trial independence. There is the situation in which a young person had a job and was let go, either for poor performance or by being laid off. And there is the situation in which they graduated from college or other training and found themselves unable to fulfill their expectation of good employment that they thought further education promised. Each experience can be formative at this young age, affecting one's faith and trust in the social system.

For the young person who is laid off, society becomes a more uncertain and scary place. As one young man asked, "How am I supposed to make my way if in whatever job I get I can be fired without cause or warning?" For the college graduate who can't find a job, much less a "good" one, there can be a sense of institutional betrayal. As one young woman attested, "I went to college to be able to get a better job, and now that I've graduated, I can't get any job. How hard is that? Plus now I'm supposed to start paying off my college loan!"

In either case, loss of position or loss of expectations, young people can experience a significant setback. Even though they are less likely at this young age to have a family to support, and the home and child-care expenses that go with that responsibility, job loss affects young people powerfully because they are just starting their journey through the world of work.

Take the case of a young woman who was at a loss to understand how her "fast-track" job could come to such a sudden halt: "I thought I was doing OK as a beginner, but I was told was that I wasn't catching on fast enough. From my college grades and my level of enthusiasm in the interview, they thought I had more skills than I did—that's what they said. When they found I didn't, they couldn't afford to take the time to train me. That's why they let me go. I tried my hardest, and it wasn't good enough. What's the matter with me? I blew a good job!"

Should parents hear such a statement, they can help with the process of explanation. For example, they might point out that there was nothing wrong with the job or with their daughter, just with the match between the two. They might say: "You might want to think of it this way. The fit was just not right. They wanted someone who could hit the ground running with very little guidance or support. Maybe that isn't the kind of job you want. Maybe what you learned is to look for a job where there's more orientation and training on the front end. Maybe slow track would work better than fast track for you. And remember: there was also incompetence on their part, too—assuming you knew more than you did. They mistook your interest and enthusiasm for your capacity to do the work without training."

By understanding the benefits of a job to young people and their feelings about the positive aspects of having a job, parents can appreciate the emotional impact of losing a job or of not being able to find one. Now you can help your child better understand why he or she is feeling down or frustrated and how to gain a better perspective that will lead not only to a new job but also to a stronger faith in their competence and potentiality. Parents can also encourage resiliency in response to receiving a setback.

RESTORING RESILIENCY

Resiliency is the capacity to rebound and recover from hardships, disappointments, and unhappy events that are a normal part of the adversities in life. For young people who had a smooth ride through the first three stages of adolescence, the loss of a job during their trial independence can pose an enormous challenge. Even after they emotionally recover from the variety of hurts that they sustained from losing a job or failing to find a job, there remains the task of gathering sufficient energy and motivation to move on and meet the challenge of employment or reemployment. This requires resiliency that parents can encourage in two ways—by *making supportive demands* and by *encouraging* a *positive attitude shift*.

First, consider the power of making supportive demands. A loss of energy can come immediately after job loss, as after any major loss. This is because recovery is so emotionally expensive. The young person has to let go of what was valued, on which many hopes and expectations may have rested, and then turn toward a future that seems daunting and scary because it is unknown.

It's this combination of loss and anxiety that can cause young people to come home and "just collapse," as these parents described the return of their twenty-two-year-old son. "He just sleeps late, lays around, hooks up with a few friends at night, comes home at all hours, and sleeps into the next day. He acts like he just doesn't want to face what he needs to do next. And we don't want to put any more pressure on him when he's obviously feeling so down. Even though we're frustrated, we want to be supportive at what we know is a hard time. So we try not to make demands on him."

But this is the wrong choice for parents. What they need to understand is that at this low-motivation, low-energy time in their child's life, parental demands can be supportive, particularly demands that can encourage getting their child into working order. To begin, parents can explain something like this:

"As far as we are concerned, your coming home needs to be a working stay, a time to get yourself back into working shape. It's not a time to come home to lick your wounds, to lay around or put off getting back on your feet. You've come back home to get in training

for the challenge ahead—to find new employment for yourself. So this is what we need from you in exchange for providing you a place to stay, which of course we are happy to do. First, you will have household membership requirements, contributions you will make to the daily running of our home. Second, you will follow a regular workweek schedule, being up and engaged with prospecting for jobs, preparing application information, submitting applications, and making interview contacts where you can. Your daily job while you are at home is looking for a job full time, putting in the same workday as we do. And third, you will end each day with a list of planned job-search activities for tomorrow, so that each day you will wake up with a constructive agenda to follow. Finally, when you do find a job, if you still want to live at home for a while, that is fine. However, at that point, we need to have you pay us some rent so you can get used to operating on a more self-supportive basis again."

It can be hard for parents going off to jobs in the morning to leave behind a college-educated son or daughter who has yet to be employed. If the search for a good job drags on, young people can feel impatient, and lack of success can drag drown their confidence and motivation. For resiliency's sake, securing some employment, no matter how unsatisfactory, creates a more affirmative mentality than having no employment at all. Thus, a part-time job, a dead-end job, or a temporary job, even a volunteer job is better than no job at all. These provide a young person with a stake in the workplace and evidence of employability.

In addition to creating supportive demands to strengthen

resiliency, parents can also encourage a positive attitude shift. It is crucial for parents to understand the negative focus that a job loss can create for their child. It is easy for the young person to become preoccupied with all that has been taken away, given up, let go, and missed, all that must be done without, and all that will never return again (at least in the same form). The more protracted the period of unemployment, the greater the danger of developing a growing feeling that one is unemployable and then losing faith in the capacities and experience one has to offer. So parents need to keep reminding the young person what those skills and past job experience are. *Resiliency requires a positive change of perspective.* Help your child understand that even the hardest times often lead to new or even better opportunities, as long as your child is open to them and looks for them in a positive way.

For example, although loss is certainly grounds for mourning, it can also be grounds for excitement once mourning has passed. *Resiliency is the capacity to turn adversity into opportunity.* Consider the young person who was laid off from the accounting job that her college major had prepared her to get:

"I'm the kind of person who just sticks to what she's got without thinking too much about it. I was always good at working with numbers, accountants work with numbers, and so why not go into accounting—that was what I figured. But what I never asked myself, until I lost this job, was this: Did I really like doing what I was naturally good at, or was there something else that I would really enjoy doing more? So I spent a couple of months doing

substitute math teaching in local middle schools just to make some money, and what I discovered was how rewarding it was to teach. The students were so much fun! It really got me excited. So that's how I discovered what I really want to do. If I hadn't gotten laid off, I would probably have spent the rest of my life keeping books, which would have been all right but certainly not the same as doing what I love. It took losing what I had to find what I was really looking for!"

RELOCATING IN THE WORKFORCE

As they learn to cope positively with unemployment, young people eventually need to work toward finding a new place for themselves in the workforce. This is often not easy, though. Two major psychological enemies of job relocation that I have seen in counseling young people are *sense of entitlement* and *intolerance of rejection*. Sometimes those go hand in hand, and sometimes not.

Entitlement is the notion that the young person deserves to get what he or she wants, including job opportunity. A sense of entitlement may come from a history of parental indulgence, from being treated as special through certain allowances and arrangements, from having a strong will that grew accustomed to getting its way, or simply from having a life in which good things just kept working out. In any case, entitlement involves the expectation that the world of work should continue to be as accommodating as family and school were while one was growing up.

For such a young person, job loss can feel like a slap in the face—not just an adversity but an affront. So a young woman, having lost one job, comes home angry at the unfairness of losing her job while others kept theirs, with the expectation that her parents will help find her another, and she awaits their assistance. But instead, her parents explain the following:

"When you were a child, you had a lot of things done for you. As an adult, you must now learn to do them for yourself. This includes finding and holding a job, and you have just experienced how uncertain keeping a job can be. That's the way life is. Not only can employment be uncertain; it can also be unfair, as you say. It's why we have each had many jobs over the years. The world doesn't owe us or you or anyone a living. You owe it to yourself to make a living and when you lose one living to find another. And we are happy to be supportive while you are doing so now."

These parents shared the reality of the adult workplace to encourage their daughter to accept that making one's adult way in the world is hard to do and that they believe she has what it takes to be able to do it.

Entitlement is not the only issue, though. Dealing with rejection can be just as tough a problem. For example, consider the young man in counseling who described just how emotionally hard coming home after a job loss can feel.

"I thought losing a job was hard, but that's nothing compared with having to look for a job again! It's like putting a 'for sale' sign on me and shopping myself around for a buyer. I feel like a

piece of damaged goods that wasn't worth that much to begin with, what with my lack of experience. The best I can find is mostly entry-level stuff. I hate putting myself out there for other people to judge, putting myself down on paper, what I've done so far (not very much!), and what I'm good at doing (also not very much). Begging for employment, that's how job hunting feels, in competition with so many other people who are better qualified. Sending off résumés and getting no reply. Making calls and nobody calls back. Either the door's not open or it's shut in my face. One rejection after another, each one proving how little I have to offer. The truth is, I'm not sure even I would hire me!"

This young man is a good example of how easy it is to get down on oneself and of how, at this vulnerable age, intolerance of rejection is a common affliction. This is why, at this time, parents can helpfully speak to their returning son or daughter about *five realities of rejection*:

1. "*Rejection should not be taken personally*. It's just a statement of disinterest in what you have to offer. Your job is to find the right job that is interested in you. Rejection by an employer does not signify anything wrong with you. It signifies only a lack of fit with what the company was looking for, or that it found among your competition someone more tailored to the job."

2. "*Rejection is not a problem; it is a reality*. Because most jobs have many applicants, most applicants will be rejected.

So you are not alone. Rejection is really just part of the selection process, during which employers sift through many applicants to find someone they feel is suited to their job."

3. *"Rejection is affirming.* You can't be rejected unless you try, so rejection affirms that you tried. The more rejections you receive signify that you are continuing to make lots of efforts on your own behalf. What is encouraging is that this shows how you possess the determination to keep trying and not give up. Tenacity is half the battle. Good for you! The will to keep applying is what it takes to land a job."

4. *"Rejection is informative.* Every time you are rejected, you have more information about the marketplace for jobs, about how to approach and not approach prospective employers, and about where your job skills and interests are more likely to find a home. So, treat job hunting as data gathering; the more approaches you make, the more knowledgeable you will grow, the more sure your search will become."

5. *"Rejection can be overcome.* There is a way to increase the likelihood of finding a job, and that is by playing the percentages and influencing the odds of acceptance in your favor. You do this by persistence and productivity. When you increase the number of applications you submit, you increase your chances. The secret of successful job relocation is continuing to show up where and when openings occur."

Teach your child about these five realities, and the instruction may take some of the threat and sting out of rejection. As rejection loses punitive or intimidating power, it becomes less likely to prevent the relocation effort that needs to get under way.

Particularly when young people return home feeling deflated from losing a job and daunted about searching for another, parents can be both coach and cheering section to help them gather the energy and determination required to get out there and try again. A simple and sincere expression of parental faith and confidence can be powerfully supportive: "You can do it!"

And if a young person who has yet to land a job returns home, understand his or her frustration. There's a trap that drives some young people to frustration: to get a job you need to have work experience, but to get work experience you need to have a job. You can't get one without the other. So what can parents advise? Without having paid job experience, what do young people have to sell a prospective employer? Volunteer work experience counts, so don't forget that. In addition, if you don't have an employment record to show what you have done, then you must put forward the qualities, interests, and capacities that define how you are a person worth hiring for the individual strengths that you possess. You have to sell yourself. One way to support that sale is to get recommendations from people who know you and support your potentiality. Some of these people may even be in a position to set up possible job contacts by putting in a good word for you.

One helpful thing I sometimes ask parents to do in counseling is to share their full employment histories with their last-stage adolescent. Seeing their parents in established occupations or careers, young people will often despair: "I can't get there from here!" That's when I ask parents to share every job they've had since high school. Then they can describe what they did and what they learned at each one, how they happened to get and leave or lose that job, how they managed periods of unemployment, how they moved on to the next job, all the way through to work they each do now.

What emerges is usually surprising to the young person. "I didn't know you did all those things! I didn't know you ever lost a job! I didn't know you ever had a hard time finding a job!" That's when parents can explain: "I didn't plan my way into different jobs. I *found* my way into different jobs—partly by looking and partly by luck. Most of it was happenstance—openings created by people who I met and the unexpected chances that came along. Just put yourself out there, knock on doors, show up on a regular basis, go after openings, take advantage of opportunities, and you'll find your way. Or because you keep yourself in public circulation, sometimes job offers will even find their way to you."

Unemployment is a difficult challenge during trial independence. It's scary when you can't find an occupational hold or lose one that you had. But with the right attitude and mentoring approach, you can help your child through this time toward a new job and a stronger sense of independence and self-worth.

PARENTING PRESCRIPTION

1. Treat looking for employment and coping with job loss as a normal, albeit hard, experience that happens to most everyone over the course of their occupational life. Empathize with and respond to the painful losses such a challenge can bring.

2. In addition to treating returning home as a "working stay," which means maintaining a normal work schedule looking for employment, support your child in maintaining a positive outlook and efforts to remain resilient.

3. Treat employment not as an entitlement but as an outcome to be earned. Help redefine rejection from feeling like a personal failure to being evidence of constructive effort.

CHAPTER SEVEN

CHALLENGE #5: ROOMMATE PROBLEMS

"I'm an only child. I grew up not having to share with anyone, used to having my space and my time to myself. The one thing I dreaded most about college was living with a roommate. To make matters worse, it would be someone I didn't even know. A stranger! As it turned out, she was perfectly nice. But there wasn't any privacy, and sometimes she'd 'borrow' without asking what I'd bought for myself. And I didn't say anything because I didn't want to make a fuss between us. I don't like conflict. Then there was more. She was up when I wanted to sleep and had friends in when I wanted time alone. She was loud and I was quiet. And she left stuff around when I needed to have things picked up. I couldn't live in a mess, and she had no need for order. It wasn't any one big thing, just a lot of little things I wasn't used to that made it so hard. But I stuck it out into the second semester; then I couldn't do it anymore. I was a wreck. I couldn't sleep and I couldn't study and I was eating just to deal with the stress. It was just too much to get used to. So I got a medical leave and came home to figure out what I was going to do."

An exciting part of the last stage of adolescence is leaving family to share living space with one or more roommates in an apartment or college dorm. Freedom has truly arrived! There are no parents to supervise or to have to answer to about what's going on. There is only the company of peers, all of whom are enjoying an exhilarating sense of independence away from home.

However, it doesn't take long for older adolescents to start appreciating the complexity of this new arrangement. Soon they discover the many unanticipated and underestimated challenges built into communal living.

Moving in with roommates seems like such an independent thing to do, and it is; but it is also an *interdependent* thing to do. In fact, it is their first attempt at creating a *domestic living arrangement or partnership*, in which two or more people share household responsibilities. Suddenly, there is intimacy with strangers or friends you didn't know on that level before. For this arrangement to work tolerably well, young people must address three hard challenges:

- Compatibility and coping with no-fault collisions
- Cooperation and managing an accidental marriage
- Communication and the necessity for speaking up

These challenges are important to face not only because, when unmet, they may cause boomerang kids to return home but also because they provide important training for how they will manage their significant live-in relationships or partnerships later on.

COMPATIBILITY AND COPING WITH NO-FAULT COLLISIONS

This first roommate experience has so much to teach. For example, when differences work well in a roommate relationship, they can become enriching, each person learning from the other an appreciation for another way of living in the world and for enjoying new life experience: "I was never exposed to adventure sports until I met my roommate, and now I love them."

However, when roommates don't share lifestyle habits, such as recreational substance use, it can be a deal breaker: "I didn't feel safe around all that alcohol use because of the wild ways it caused my roommate and her friends to behave." Talk with some veterans of the first-roommate wars, and horror stories about serious incompatibilities abound. There's the roommate "from hell" who was insensitive, offensive, irresponsible, troublesome, tempestuous, or even dangerous to live with. For example, rooming with someone who has been repressed by too many home rules or undisciplined by too few may lead to a wild ride, with one roommate wanting to let go of all control and the other holding on for dear life.

Even without any extreme problems, however, the first communal living experience can be jarring. Why? Because people are different in myriad ways, and many of those differences do not mesh well or match up when roommates move in together. These differences can be linked to lifestyle (values, tastes, and habits), psychological makeup (personality, temperament, and functioning), and motivation (wants, preferences, and interests).

Whatever the source of the problem, parents can explain how these human differences demand adjustment to live with and are sometimes a source of irritation or offense for both parties. So when their son complains about how hard one of his roommates is to live with, his parents can talk about *no-fault collisions*—inevitable incompatibilities in relationships for which nobody is to blame and that everybody must learn to put up with. When young people return to live at home because they couldn't get along with roommates, while empathizing with the situation, parents can do some coaching about tolerating and working with interpersonal diversity.

Of course, those young people with the least experience with diversity often have the most to learn and get used to when taking on a roommate. Thus, a young person who grew up socially sheltered by sticking to the same small clique of similar friends in middle school and high school may find accommodating individual differences with roommates particularly hard. Parents can suggest how this hardship always cuts two ways—each person presents differences with which the other person is unfamiliar and can find difficult to get along: "The problem is not just that she is different from you; you are equally different from her. You are different from each other." Further, parents can point out that all relationships must encompass some of these differences, and that the more independence broadens one's life experience, the more interpersonal diversity will be encountered.

Roommate differences create a sense of contrast that can cause young people to feel incompatible, such as, "We don't like the same kind of music." And although difference in musical tastes might seem trivial, when you're sharing the same living space and exposed to what you don't like hearing at high volume, the difference becomes amplified in importance. And when that musical taste is also linked to a cultural affiliation or identification, the difference can come to represent even more: "She's so country, and I'm much more into rock," for example. Continually taking offense at this no-fault collision, young people complain, "This person is impossible to live with!"

Consider just a few common no-fault collisions between roommates on a variety of topics:

- *Privacy*: "She listens when I'm talking to my boyfriend on the phone."
- *Order*: "He hates picking up, and I hate a mess."
- *Reliability*: "I have to bug her for the rent money or she forgets."
- *Personality*: "I like time to myself, and he wants constant company."
- *Entertainment*: "She wants the TV always on, and I like it sometimes off."
- *Computer use*: "He's gaming all the time, so he's never really there."
- *Socializing*: "Her friends come over all hours of the day and night."
- *Substance use*: "He promised he didn't smoke, but apparently that didn't include pot."

- *Hygiene*: "My roommate smells because she refuses to take a daily shower."
- *Bill paying*: "He wanted cable, I didn't; he got it and expects me to pay."
- *Housekeeping*: "I feel like her parent, nagging her to throw out her trash."
- *Goals*: "I'm focused on my future, and he just wants to party."
- *Communication*: "She won't discuss disagreements, so nothing gets settled."
- *Values*: "He cracks mean jokes about groups of people that I don't find funny."

The lesson is that there are many different ways roommates may come into conflict. Even friends (much less acquaintances or strangers) do not automatically make good roommates. It takes a lot of effort by all concerned to get along.

People are simply different in a host of ways. So incompatibilities in roommate relationships are not really a problem; they are a reality. The challenge is how to manage those inevitable incompatibilities. Parents can offer some suggestions—either before or after the problem has come to a head—to help their child learn some important life lessons from the experience.

To achieve compatibility around *differences that can't be changed* (like personality, functioning, and values) requires understanding, tolerance, and acceptance, and making respectful room for the differences between you. So to manage a relationship in which one roommate stays up late (a "night person") and the other gets up early (a "morning person"), both should try to keep it quiet when the other is asleep. In that way, both make mutual accommodation to a functional difference. Acting judgmentally, critically, and with blame are the enemies of acceptance and respect.

To achieve compatibility around *differences that can be changed* (like preferences, wants, and habits) requires speaking up, discussing, and negotiating to modify the differences between the roommates. For example, roommates who have differences about the importance of keeping the kitchen, bathroom, and common room picked up can agree on a cleanup every couple of days—not as regularly as one roommate would find ideally orderly, but more regularly than the other would find ideally relaxing. In that way, both roommates have made an accommodation to a difference in preferences. Acting in a controlling, commanding, or coercive way is the enemy of discussion and negotiation.

The more difficult differences, though, are the ones that are unchangeable. A particularly intractable set of roommate conflicts can arise from incompatibility that is based on similarity. This is how one young man described it to me:

"We just kept butting heads, Chris and me. Right from the start. At first I thought it was because we were so different, but I think now we were too alike. We are both ultracompetitive. We both have to be in control, to win, and to be right. And of course, neither one of us will back down. Plus, there was nothing so small that it didn't matter. We're both detail people. So it was one endless argument with no letup or peace between us. We had two other roommates, and

I think we drove them crazy. Our arguing never stopped. Finally, it got so bad that it was a war between enemies about who would be in charge of every little thing. It got pretty emotional and intense. Although we never came to blows, our words did a lot of damage. At the end of the semester, I needed to come home and rethink living with a roommate. I don't know what happened to him."

Another main cause of unchangeable conflicts are differences in beliefs and values. In such a case, it's unlikely that one person will change a deeply held belief just to accommodate the other. So the very liberal and the very conservative student roommates at first clash over their politics; the more they argue, the righter each one feels, and the more polarized the relationship becomes. At last, to preserve peace between them, they decide to leave political differences alone.

Even very objectionable unchangeable differences can be accommodated and adjusted to if roommates focus on changing how these differences are managed. For example, take a value difference, such as the young person who really didn't like how his roommate liked to make mean jokes about groups of people. In this case, parents might suggest: "Ask your roommate to please not tell those kinds of insulting jokes in your presence. When he agrees, you don't have to deal with them, even if the difference between each of you remains unaltered." Acting adamantly, rigidly, and inflexibly are the enemies of adjustment and accommodation.

The more kinds of no-fault collisions occur, though, the more challenging the relationship usually is. So if a roommate relationship requires accepting more incompatibilities than a young person can tolerate and sends him or her packing for home, how can parents help their child learn from that experience?

First, you have to listen to your child's story. For example, a parent may hear this:

> *"Of the three roommates, I don't know who was worse for me. There was the one whose boyfriend was a nonpaying boarder, at least at night, and they never wanted to be disturbed. There was the one who just used the apartment to dump and run, leaving her stuff thrown anywhere, in a rush out the door. Or the one who was finally free from some strict parents and determined to take advantage of that freedom—at all hours of the day or night. I'd come in after classes and never know who or how many people I would find or what kind of a good time they were having. I think sharing the apartment worked for each of them, but for me it was total chaos. One thing all three had in common—they never had time to listen to me. They weren't mean about it, just too busy. 'We'll talk later, Caroline,' they'd promise. But we never did. I finally decided I needed order, quiet, and sanity. That's why I came back home."*

In this case, the young woman was not overreacting. A first apartment can be life in the fast lane for many young people, and if that's not what they want, that's not the place they should be. Beyond that, Caroline was pretty accepting of the nest of differences she was living in, but she decided that the living conditions those differences created were not OK with her. And young people with roommate difficulties need to evaluate the incompatible differences and the effect that they have on their lives. In the case of Caroline, the apartment was host to four people with distinct lifestyles that were not likely to change. For the three other roommates, the differences were not a problem, but for Caroline, they were because the difference they made in her life proved unworkable.

Good roommate relationships require some minimal compatibility, which was lacking in Caroline's case. Parents might suggest that their child do an adequate prescreening of a roommate next time around. To determine suitability, the roommates might pose some significant questions to each other:

- "Have either one of us roomed with anyone before, and if so, have we learned any helpful lessons about getting along?"
- "What are significant differences between us, and what difficulty might these differences cause?"
- "What are some possibly hard-to-live-with personal characteristics and habits that we each bring to the roommate relationship?"
- "What do we want and not want the apartment to be used for?"
- "What basic household rules would we like to see in place?"
- "What are the most important responsibilities we need each other to take?"
- "What kinds of courtesy (small acts of consideration) would each of us really appreciate?"

- "When any part of our living arrangements is not working for either of us, how are we going to let the other know so we can talk and work it out?"

With many, if not most, first-roommate experiences, a lot of no-fault collisions are the order of the day. The most important thing a young person—and his or her parents—can do is to learn which incompatible differences to work through and negotiate, which ones to work around and accept, and which ones make the relationship insupportable.

COOPERATION AND MANAGING AN ACCIDENTAL MARRIAGE

Most new roommates don't anticipate how sharing the same living space and having to cooperate to manage joint responsibility creates an *accidental marriage* between them. By setting up house together, the roommates create a kind of *domestic partnership*. As in an actual marriage, their interdependence and reliance on each other affect the well-being of each one. For daily interdependence to work well, it takes cooperation, cooperation requires sharing, and sharing means dividing up and taking turns and letting each other use what two parties jointly possess as a function of now living together. On every human level, having to cooperate is challenging, whether it be between siblings, between marriage partners, between countries, or between roommates.

In the excitement of moving out, though, most young people

don't anticipate this sort of thing being a problem. Before they have to do it, sharing sounds simple ("We just divide what is separately ours and share what we have in common") and cooperation sounds easy ("We just rely on each other to make things work").

Entwined in each other's lives, however, they must make living arrangements that work for each one and for them both, and that is no easy task. This is why cooperation is required. When sharing arrangements are not satisfactory for all concerned, the opportunity for conflict can arise. To see how, just consider some simple but potentially divisive questions that roommates have to answer when they move in together:

- Who gets to get what? (Choosing a bedroom)
- Who gets to do what? (Dealing with the landlord)
- Who gets to control what? (Setting the TV schedule)
- Whose way is the right way? (Arranging the furniture)
- What is a fair share? (Determining housekeeping responsibility)
- What is best use? (Dividing up the spare closet)
- How to take turns? (Using the washer and dryer)
- What decisions are to be jointly made? (Having a party)
- What decisions are to be individually made? (Setting one's personal schedule)

In answering these and other questions about cooperation, disagreement will naturally arise. When it does, engaging in conflict does not simply mean that the roommates do not get along; conflict becomes the communication process that helps them get along when confronting, discussing, and resolving points of opposition between them.

At best, conflict allows roommates to bridge their differences. They can gain more understanding of each other by hearing each other out, and they can become more unified with each other by reaching an agreement that each party can support. In doing so, they strengthen the relationship on both counts, an important skill they will carry forward into later domestic partnerships of a romantic kind.

Most young people, though, never having had to deal with it before, are unskilled at dealing with conflict with a roommate. So when conflict arises, they immediately think of three options:

- My way (domineer)
- Your way (surrender)
- No way (maintain disagreement)

They don't consider the fourth way: our way (collaborate).

Parents can help explain the complexity of this situation, and on the basis of their own marital or other experiences, they can offer strategies for making cooperation work. When a roommate conflict comes up, parents can play a useful role in identifying what caused the problem and in suggesting what might have not worked and what might work better the next time around. For example, a young man might say: "We just keep fighting about household responsibilities. We each feel we are doing more than the other guy." That's when one of the parents can reach back into personal history to retrieve this idea: "I can remember breaking that tension with a roommate long ago. We worked out a chore wheel of rotating responsibilities. It took some talking, but it really helped organize housekeeping and took a lot of possible disagreements off the table."

As a parent, you can recommend three collaborative rules for dealing with conflicts, ones that not only can resolve the conflict but also help strengthen the roommate relationship:

1. *Compromise*—One can try to compromise by *working through* a difference and trying to establish a middle ground: "If we each give a little, maybe we can settle our difference by each getting some of what we want. You can have the apartment for your socializing at night, if you are willing to keep it quiet for my studying in the morning."

2. *Concession*—One can try concession by *working around* the difference: "This time I'll go with what you want because I think the issue is more important to you than to me. I don't want a cat, but you really do, and I can live with the decision to have a pet."

3. *Equity*—Both parties can commit to the *rule of equity*: "When we compromise, we both sacrifice some of what we ideally want, and when we concede, we each make that sacrifice about the same proportion of times. This way the balance of getting and giving in to get along feels fair."

Parents can help their child evaluate how well the inherent conflicts of cooperation were managed by asking the following:

- "How well were you able to compromise?"
- "How well were you able to make concessions?"
- "How well were you able to manage compromise and concession in a manner that felt equitable to you both?"

Implicit in this last question is an evaluation of the process upon which compromise and concession must depend: communication. Communication is the key to making any good relationship work, as we'll examine in the next section.

COMMUNICATION AND THE NEED TO SPEAK UP

Differences become most difficult when roommates, one or both, elect not to communicate about them.

Why would they not? They may have come out of a family where engaging in conflict didn't feel acceptable or safe. Or in early conflict with the roommate, communication may have been intense, angry, belittling, blaming, critical, threatening, or otherwise uncomfortable. If this last condition is true, then before roommates can constructively take on the conflict, they must address the process of communication. One young man did it this way: he explained to his yelling roommate, "I can't understand when you talk so loud, but I would like to know what you have to say. To discuss this disagreement, I need for us to do it in a calm, quiet, and reasoned way."

When it comes to conflict in roommate relationships, there are a few important realities to communication:

- Speak up, and your needs will be known.
- Keep quiet, and your needs will be unknown.
- Delay speaking up, and you risk building up hurt or anger about what is going on.

The last one is key: probably the most important communication commitment roommates can make to each other is to *timeliness*. A lot of differences can become worse when roommates avoid communication and allow feelings of hurt and offense to build up. Then, when they finally address the issue, it has become too big to ignore, grievance and resentment generate accusation and blame, and defensiveness destroys meaningful discussion. So parents couched their advice in terms for what worked for them in marriage. "We have found that a great way to avoid this problem is to make a rule. Whenever either of us has issues with the other's conduct, responsibilities, or living arrangements in general, the concerned party will *speak up* about it in specific terms and the other person will hear the other out. Then both of us commit to a time when we will work the issue or disagreement out. This may be right now or, if one of us is really upset, it may be a little later." Lessons from the adult marriage (domestic partnership) can have a lot to teach a son or daughter about managing roommate relationships.

Parents can also honor the reality that speaking up in a relationship does not always feel easy or comfortable to do. They can explain some of the challenges involved. Speaking up in a relationship means to reveal something about who one is, how one feels, what one wants, which way works best, and why one is acting or reacting in a certain way. Consider five positive reasons to encourage young people to speak up:

1. To *express* their feelings and communicate their experience, managing pressures and problems best when they can talk them out
2. To *explain* their needs and point of view to be understood, stating their case and letting others know what they think
3. To *question* others to find out what's happening, asking about what they want to learn about or need to know
4. To *confront* others after being hurt or wronged, using words to set limits to protect themselves from treatment that is not OK
5. To *resolve* differences and to settle conflicts, using communication to work out disagreements

The problem, though, is that all five of these reasons can be hard for last-stage adolescents to do. For example, in this stage, adolescents may be reluctant to do the following:

- To *express* themselves, because doing so may expose vulnerability and sensitivity and create embarrassment
- To *explain* themselves, because they might face disapproval, have to defend their view or opinion, or back down
- To *question*, because it can expose ignorance in them that others might tease or criticize
- To *confront*, because others might use that stand to attack them even more

- To try to *resolve* a disagreement, because they would rather avoid the emotional discomfort of conflict

Speaking up is hard to do because a lot is at stake. But for the same reason, it is important to do. If young people haven't already learned to speak up at home, doing so with roommates is a great chance to learn this skill. Through speaking up, the young person asserts self-definition, which allows him or her to become publicly known.

To appreciate the importance of this ability to communicate, consider what happens to young people who, rather than speak up, learn to stay silent:

- Instead of expressing themselves, they conceal their thoughts and feelings.
- Instead of explaining themselves, they keep their opinions to themselves and defer to what others have to say.
- Instead of questioning others, they learn to live with ignorance, anxiously awaiting what to be told, leaving that up to others.
- Instead of confronting mistreatment, they dare take no stands when hurt or wronged, inviting mistreatment to continue.
- Instead of engaging in disagreement, they avoid conflict at all costs, leaving important differences unresolved.

In the daily transactions of roommate life, silent people are at a huge disadvantage. They can't express feelings or wants or opinions or limits or needs. They can't assert self-interest or dissent to protect it. The silent person is in danger of living too much on other people's terms.

So when a daughter returns to live at home, filled with blame for her roommates for being so unmindful of her needs, so insensitive to her feelings, so bossy to be around, and so unwilling to share what was held in common, parents are right to be concerned. They can ask, "Did you speak up about what you wanted and didn't want to happen, about what you needed them to know, about when you disagreed?" And her reply might be a telling one: "I didn't feel OK saying anything. I felt too uncomfortable."

So parents, do your adolescents a favor when they're growing up at home with you. Encourage them to speak up. Don't discourage argumentative communication by treating it as talking back. Don't favor their being quiet because you like the silent compliance. In counseling, I've seen that those young people who learned to keep silent growing up have a much harder time creating workable roommate relationships than those who have learned to speak up on their own behalf. In general, it usually works out better for someone to be socially outspoken in life than to be socially silent. Shy people, for example, not only suffer in silence; they suffer *from* silence. They need encouragement to gather the courage to define and declare themselves by daring to speak up. By helping them learn that speaking up is not only OK but also important, you will help them learn to communicate not only with roommates, but also in any significant relationships that come their way.

GETTING READY FOR A ROOMMATE AGAIN

When a roommate relationship becomes so strained that a young person leaves and returns to live at home, it usually means one of the following five things:

1. Incompatibilities could not be tolerated.
2. Cooperation could not be established.
3. Communication has broken down.
4. Conflicts could not be resolved.
5. Some combination of the first four has occurred.

The most important thing parents can do is help their child debrief the unhappy experience in order to learn some painful lessons:

- "I need to admit that I'm not that easiest person to live with either."
- "I need to be better at working out disagreements."
- "I need to speak up more to let other people know what I am feeling and wanting."
- "I'll be better prepared for my next roommate experience now."

Once your child knows why roommate conflicts occur and how best to handle them, he or she will be ready to take on the benefits of living with a roommate and have the skills to make it work.

PARENTING PRESCRIPTION

1. Explain to your child that roommate relationships are difficult because they are usually a young person's first attempt to manage a domestic partnership arrangement, with all the challenges of cooperation, incompatibilities, and conflicts that sharing household responsibilities can bring.

2. However bad a roommate experience is, your child needs to evaluate how more tolerance of differences and tact in addressing them might help the relationship work better, as might distinguishing differences that can be changed from those that cannot.

3. Help your child understand how important it is to speak up when the roommate relationship is not working, and how to cooperatively use compromise, concession, and equity to work through disagreement.

CHAPTER EIGHT

CHALLENGE #6: BROKEN LOVE RELATIONSHIPS

"We lived together for almost two years and I was really in love with her. Maybe I loved her too much, because I started paying more of her expenses and even signed for some of her debt. I'd never been in love before, and I just figured this was it. Someday we'd get married and live happily ever after—that was how I felt. But she was more experienced in relationships than me. I don't think she was trying to use me. She just got tired of me as the magic wore off, at least for her. Then she wanted more of a separate social life, and pretty soon that included guys. Finally, one day she left, and it took everything out of me. I didn't want to live in that place anymore. I could barely make it to my job. I just needed a break. So I came home."

I don't know how many young people actually fall in love in high school, but on the basis of my counseling experience with adolescents, I would guess that it's a small minority. The chemistry of falling into romantic love—attraction, infatuation, loving companionship, and emotional intimacy that increases one's capacity for attachment—happens to relatively few high school teens.

Come trial independence, however, the susceptibility of older adolescents to falling in love increases, because they are away from home, feel more socially alone, are more mature, and have grown more open to the possibility of romantic companionship to help anchor themselves when they are out on their own. Feeling less connected to family and old friends can create more openness to loving companionship.

However, the eventual breakup of a relationship can be devastating, particularly when it is the *first* love. In that case, a young person may suddenly want to return to the sanctuary of home to put the shattered pieces of his or her life back together.

When failed love breaks the heart of young people shortly after they have stepped out on their own, they face three big challenges in recovering:

1. Dealing with rejection
2. Identifying varieties of losses
3. Assessing the relationship

In this painful process, with understanding and guidance, parents can be of help, either after their child boomerangs home or before, to help them recover.

DEALING WITH REJECTION

In a breakup, just as in a divorce, unless the separation is mutually desired (with both partners sharing the hardship of the decision), there will be two roles to play, one more painful than the other. One role to play is *initiator*, the partner who has thought it over, felt it through, and decided to end the relationship. The other role to play is the *reactor*, the partner who expects or wants the relationship to continue and may be surprised and hurt by the decision to end it.

Each role brings with it emotional burdens. The initiator bears the responsibility for terminating the relationship and the *guilt* for causing the reactor to suffer. The reactor must bear the *rejection* of being cast aside.

In most cases, when a breakup causes a young person to return home, that son or daughter is usually the reactor. Thus, parents' concern should be helping manage rejection and hurt. The key question for parents to ask is this: "Is our child taking the rejection personally?" It's one thing to feel emotionally wounded by the loss, but it is another to blame the broken relationship on a personal failing or inadequacy and then reject oneself. This creates a double dose of pain, and self-esteem can plummet.

As one young man despaired to his parents, "What's wrong with me when the person I love can suddenly stop loving me?"

"What can we tell our son?" they asked. "We just hate to see him beat up on himself on top of being broken-hearted. It's like punishing himself for getting hurt!"

There are a number of valuable distinctions that parents can suggest to moderate the pain their child is feeling:

- "Just because the other person has lost interest in you doesn't mean that you have lost worth."
- "Just because the relationship doesn't work anymore for the other person doesn't mean there is something wrong with you; something has changed in them."
- "Just because the other person broke his or her loving commitment to you doesn't mean you should break that commitment to yourself."
- "Just because it feels like this is your loss alone doesn't mean that it is not the other person's loss, too—you have both lost something precious you once shared."
- "Just because the other person no longer values continuing the relationship doesn't mean that the relationship did not have value."
- "Just because the other person's love didn't last forever doesn't mean that once upon a time love was not there."
- "Just because the other person can live happily without you doesn't mean that, in time, you cannot come to live happily without him or her."
- "Just because the other person ended the relationship doesn't mean that your life is coming to an end, only to a turning point."
- "Just because the other person has lost love for you doesn't mean you will not be able, in time, to find new love with someone else."

- "Just because you learned that the person you love the most can hurt you the worst doesn't mean you should never risk loving again."
- "Most important, just because you dared to give your heart and have it broken doesn't mean the love was not of lasting value: you carry forward courage that one day will allow you to love again."

By talking them through these understandings, parents can help their bereaved sons or daughters to not give rejection a lasting, wounding power. And then they will be that much closer to opening up to a loving relationship again should the opportunity arise.

IDENTIFYING VARIETIES OF LOSS

Just as job loss creates a multitude of psychological losses to deal with (see Chapter 6), broken love relationships create multiple losses, too. Each of these losses is marked by questions that need answering if the young person (the one rejected and returning home) can come to terms with emotional acceptance of the breakup and be able to move on. The following sections discuss a variety of common losses that a breakup can create.

Loss of Understanding

Breakup always creates the need for information in the rejected party. The question is: "Why did the other person want to end the relationship with me?" Often, the young person has no good explanation for the breakup because the initiator chose not to tell.

I once worked with a young man in counseling who was truly bewildered:

"I didn't even know anything was wrong. I literally got a 'Dear John' letter. That was all. She wrote, 'After much thought, I believe we should stop seeing each other. Of course I wish you the best. Katherine.' No more 'Kate.' Two years and that's how it ends? What am I supposed to think? She wouldn't even answer my emails or return my calls. My parents suggested I send a letter and say that I will respect her wishes but would like to ask, 'for the sake of the love we shared, to give me some explanation for your change of heart, because that would really help me let go and move on.'"

I told the young man that I thought his parents had a good idea and that I supported what they had suggested. Better to be painfully enlightened than be left to his own dark imaginings, wondering what he had done wrong. And she did write back, confessing that an old boyfriend had come back into the picture, and it was with that person that she wanted to spend her time. When it comes to breakups, a painful explanation is usually better than none at all, even if what one did or didn't do contributed to the loss.

Loss of Future

Breakup not only severs an attachment now, but it also ends expectations for the relationship later on. The question is, "What will I do with my life now?" The couple had plans they had talked about, all that they would do and share together. They had set an agenda for the future. When that agenda is gone, the young person may look at the emptiness ahead and wonder about what happens next.

Understanding that your son or daughter is at a transition point, not knowing how to navigate through it, and you can provide a framework for them to be able to conceive of a helpful transition. Your job is not to argue against the painful part of loss but to point out the gainful part. And that gainful part is this: *the other side of loss is freedom.*

How can this be? Because with the condition and circumstance of the old relationship no longer standing, two new freedoms have been created—*freedom from old demands and restraints* and *freedom for new choices and opportunities.*

This is the focus parents need to encourage their child. And they can do so by asking two questions. The *freedom from old demands and restraints* question is: "What old conditions and constraints are you now free to do without?" For *freedom for new choices and opportunities*, the question is: "What interests, possibilities, relationships, and opportunities are you now free to explore?"

So, for example, parents might suggest: "Now you are free from keeping your ex informed about your comings and goings as well as the necessity for joint decision making. And now you are free to do whatever you'd like and to see whomever you would like whenever you like." Pointing out these new freedoms will help young people begin to envision a positive future ahead.

Parents can also mention that many first love relationships break up because for the initiating party, commitment creates a loss of personal freedom, and breaking up restores that freedom. So the breakup was motivated less by not liking things about the other person than simply by the desire to be "free" again. He or she was simply not ready to settle down.

Loss of Companionship

Breakup causes the rejected party to feel solitary. The question here is, "Since we're no longer together, who will I be with now?"

Being in love can actually be socially isolating. Often young people make the relationship a focus of social attention, to the exclusion of everyone else. One young woman explained:

"With someone right there, I got lazy about seeing other people. Plus being a couple for so long became who I was. 'We' did everything together, and when people thought of me, they thought of 'us.' We were just part of each other, and it's only now without him that I realize how much of my social life I've given up. Friends just got tired of calling, and a few of them got hurt when I acted like I didn't want to spend as much time with them as they (and I) were used to. So now I'm single again and totally out of the social swim. It feels like starting over. I feel so alone!"

And what she didn't say was that it felt awkward, even scary.

In this situation, as a parent you can acknowledge the challenge of getting back into the social circle. You can empathize with this being hard to do when, in addition to feeling out of practice, the young person's confidence is lowered from the aftereffects of rejection. Then you can encourage your child to join some organized interest or activity groups, to attend gatherings to revive his or her socializing skills, to call up old friends and acquaintances who have fallen away, and even to initiate and accept casual dating. And of course, there is always social networking on the Internet. Having taken oneself out of social circulation for the sake of the old relationship, now the task is to get oneself back in.

Loss of Adequacy

Breakup often causes the rejected party to criticize him- or herself. The question here is, "What is wrong with me?"

As mentioned earlier, it is hard for a person to be rejected without, to some degree, worsening the painful experience by faulting oneself. Assessing and assigning one's share of responsibility for the loss of relationship is one thing, but running oneself down is another. Beating up on oneself in the wake of a breakup, when one is already going through a bad time, is a bad idea. In fact, one needs to boost one's own sense of worth.

So in this case, you can encourage young people to ask and answer the counterquestion: "What is *right* with me?" By affirming themselves with positive thoughts, setting positive expectations for themselves, and engaging in self-enhancing activities, they can restore their sense of personal adequacy. And if the young person is so sad that she is unable to identify positive and attractive aspects of herself, parents can offer to itemize those positives themselves.

Recovering

Parents will know that recovery is under way when they start to hear statements of letting go, such as the following:

- "I'm starting to feel better."
- "I have some things I'm looking forward to."
- "Maybe the bad was for the best."
- "I'm ready to move on."
- "I don't think about her (or him) much anymore."

But parents will know that their child is still holding on from such statements as these:

- "I can't stop missing what we had."
- "I still believe we'll get back together."
- "I'll keep on loving him [or her] no matter what."

If after several months at home the young person is still sounding stuck, it is usually advisable to find him or her some counseling to help move through what is still a very painful loss. Counseling can help with letting go.

One of the toughest jobs for parents is hanging in there with their son or daughter when a breakup keeps mending and then breaking off again. The young person vacillates between letting go and holding on, enduring loss and embracing hope, giving up and wanting to give it another try, cutting off and then getting back in contact. Why? Even for the party doing the jilting, the relationship was not an entirely unhappy experience. In fact, because the couple shared many good times as well, it is easy to shift from focusing on what didn't work in the relationship to what did, and this shift creates the on-again and off-again tug-of-war that parents can find so frustrating to watch. "Why can't she just make up her mind?"

Help your child understand that breaking up in most cases is not the outcome of a single decision. It is often a process of extended internal debate over the pros and cons of maintaining or ending a very powerful relationship in which the possibility of lasting love is at stake. In this process, young people can feel painfully torn whichever way they choose, so any "final" choices are going to be hard come by. Thus, parents have to be patient while this heartrending deliberation unfolds. One of the great benefits of moving back home after a breakup is that it can provide a young person with separation, distance, and perspective, all of which allow for a more reflective and objective point of view to prevail, free from the daily pressure of the relationship.

To the degree that they are invited to participate in this deliberation, parents can reflect back what the young person has told them about the relationship to bring back into focus what the specific salient events and experiences were like. A lot of times their reminder can help a young person stick to a decision. So they can say, "You told us that, love you as he said he did and says he does, he still strayed into other intimacies, so you might want to remember that."

You can also help your son or daughter gain from the education the breakup had to teach about how to assess the quality of a caring relationship.

ASSESSING THE RELATIONSHIP

When parents can provide some guidelines for evaluating the "goodness" of a lost relationship, they can help influence how their child selects a companion in his or her next relationship.

In what ways did the relationship work well and in what ways did it work badly? What kind of treatment has their child learned to expect in a relationship, and what unhealthy behavior does he or she not want? These questions help young people evaluate their relationships for lessons that can make the next relationship better. Parents need to be realistic about relationship education. It is not addressed in school. It is a product of life experience. So here, parents can be very helpful in sorting out the breakup experience.

For example, they can suggest four simple questions to which a son or daughter needs to answer yes, to affirm that the relationship was good, or at least good enough:

- *Did I like how I treated myself in the relationship?* For example, was it an equal relationship? Did my needs and wants count for as much as the other person's?
- *Did I like how I treated the other person in the relationship?* For example, was I tolerant? Did I accept the right of the other person to view things differently from me?
- *Did I like how the other person treated me in the relationship?* For example, was there respect? Did the other person accept disagreement without criticizing or pushing me to change my mind?
- *Did I like how the other person treated him- or herself in the relationship?* For example, was there forbearance? Did the other person manage frustration, failure, or disappointment calmly, without becoming angry or upset with him- or herself?

If a young person cannot answer yes to all four questions, then there is some work to do on developing a healthy relationship. For many young people, the path to learning how to have a good relationship runs through the hard experience of having one or more bad relationships. In the words of one veteran of an unhappy love experience, "I never want to fall for anyone like that again!" So the more young people are able to evaluate their relationships honestly, the better prepared they will be for the next relationship they enter.

If you find that your child is engaged in and does well with this idea of evaluating their relationships, there are more specific, advanced questions you can suggest that he or she think about as well, ones that are relevant for couples of any age:

- *Expression*: "Did you both feel free to speak up about what matters?"
- *Attention*: "Did you both feel listened to when expressing a concern?"
- *Security*: "Did you both feel that the comfort and safety limits each person set were observed?"
- *Conflict*: "Did you feel disagreement was managed so that neither of you felt emotionally or physically threatened and that differences got resolved?"
- *Commitment*: "Did you both keep promises and agreements that were made?"
- *Honesty*: "Did you both trust each other to tell the truth, and was the truth told?"
- *Independence*: "Did you both support each other's having separate time apart?"
- *Anger*: "Did you both express and respond to an offense or violation so you could talk it out and work it out peacefully, not aggressively?"
- *Fairness*: "Did you both evenly share effort and responsibility so neither one did most of the giving or getting?"
- *Communication*: "Did you both speak up to keep each other adequately informed?"

Factoring in these advanced questions shows how it takes a lot of work to create a love relationship in which both parties can answer yes to all these questions.

DIFFICULT SITUATIONS

One thing you never want is for your son or daughter to be treated meanly in a relationship. But if that should occur, it becomes worse if your child does not speak up about it, accepts or makes excuses for it, or worst of all believes it is deserved.

If you hear expressions of the *mistreatment mind-set*, you need to pay heed. There are six beliefs that can support this mind-set:

1. "I don't deserve to be treated well."
2. "If I act really good, I won't be treated badly."
3. "If I am treated badly, it's because I wasn't acting good enough."
4. "If I love enough, I can change the other person and his or her mistreating ways."
5. "If the other person promises not to hurt me again, I need to forgive and forget."
6. "If I lose this person's love, I will never find another, so I must make the best of what I get."

If parents hear any statements like these, they should encourage their child to get psychological help so that the next relationship has a possibility of being a healthier one. Many young people do suffer through a bad relationship, in which they are treated badly or act badly themselves, before they learn enough to create a good relationship in which both parties are treated well. But this improvement can occur only if he or she learns constructive lessons along the way.

Another difficult situation occurs when a breakup is complicated by unintentional pregnancy. Then very serious responsibilities need to be fully discussed. In trial independence, there is a resurgence among adolescents in believing that one doesn't have to play by the rules (like using protections when engaging in sex) and acting more unmindfully of consequences. The reality of pregnancy brings grown-up responsibility back into sudden focus. Getting a counselor to help sort through the complexity can be helpful.

HELPING THEM TO LOVE AGAIN

Many parents worry about how or whether to help their child through a breakup, understanding that it is not their job to manage a son's or daughter's relationship. But although it isn't parents' job to manage, they can mentor young people by providing them with important questions to ask themselves. What you want is for your child to learn from the experience more about what it means and what it takes to have a good relationship, so that he or she is more likely and able to have a well-working committed partnership later on. Most important, you want your son or daughter to appreciate that, although the breakup hurts, it doesn't nullify the good that was there. Just as the bad does not have to be repeated, what was good can carry over to build on in another relationship.

And most important, you want your young person to understand that loving someone, or getting love from someone, is never a good substitute for loving oneself.

PARENTING PRESCRIPTION

1. If your child is the jilted party, help him or her to not take this rejection personally or to self-reject.

2. After empathizing with the pain of loss, help your child explore and appreciate how the other side of loss creates freedoms one didn't have before.

3. Help your child evaluate and draw lessons from the lost relationship that will help him or her better select, understand, and grow in future relationships.

CHAPTER NINE

CHALLENGE #7: SUBSTANCE USE

"I didn't drink every day like a lot of my friends. But when I did drink I always did it to get drunk. Sometimes, I guess I was pretty funny, at least that's what they told me. Sometimes I didn't remember, except waking up the next morning with a headache that wouldn't quit. But then I got the DWI [driving-while-intoxicated violation], and my parents found out. And then about all the other drinking. Who told them, I don't know—maybe someone minding my business, maybe my friends? My folks had been preaching against my drinking for years, telling me stories about my dad's brother and my mom's mom, and all the damage drinking did. I wasn't paying that much attention. What did they know? Then they pulled me up short. I was still getting some housing and living allowance, but they cut that off. That's when they offered me this deal. Come back home, get my drinking assessed, and maybe go to treatment, or I would be on my own. So I came home."

During trial independence, young people have the freedom to live away from home *free* from what parents can say, see, supervise, and know. But moving out creates a mixed blessing. Living on one's own often feels lonelier and more disconnected than living at home, and older adolescents can find themselves desperately floundering to become socially established in a new setting. *The combination of new freedom and new social urgency are what make trial independence a more impulsive age, the one during which substance use is most widespread and often heaviest of all.*

As a parent, then, it is important to understand three challenges that late-stage adolescents face in managing safe substance use in a drug-filled world:

1. Understanding how substance use can cause problems
2. Recognizing signs of trouble with substances
3. Getting help for substance abuse

SUBSTANCE USE AND THE PROBLEMS IT CAUSES

All substance use is about satisfying the desire for freedom—the freedom *from* negative feelings (escape) or *for* positive affect (pleasure). The problem is that this chemically induced freedom comes at a cost: freedom from sober caring.

With freedom from caring, as the young person becomes more drug- or alcohol-affected, he or she cares less; acts more careless; and in the extreme (drunk or wasted), feels free to think and feel and act as though he or she doesn't care at all. The young person operates impulsively, abandoning what he or she would normally, soberly, care about. The rule of reason, principles, cautions, past lessons, and future consequences are of no concern. Only the moment matters. In this altered state, young people can make decisions that they (and maybe others) will later regret. Then, afterward, when the intoxication has long worn off, the young person is left to confront and pay the price of that drug-induced freedom. Like one young woman recalled a week after her drunken adventure: "It was a fraternity party. I was only caring about what felt exciting now. What could happen later never crossed my mind. But later has happened. I guess it always does."

During trial independence, young people have a lot of opportunity to encounter substances, given the increase in parties that go on during this stage. Away from home, parties provide a social vehicle for hanging out, meeting people, acting more adult, and making new relationships. And this is where "get-to-know-you drugs," particularly alcohol, come into play, providing the "liquid courage" to loosen up and feel less self-conscious and more confident about how one looks, how one acts, and what one says. It's no fun partying while anxious. For many young people, substance use on these occasions feels required for the sake of personal comfort and fitting in socially. *Partying*, in fact, is also a term for situations in which excessive drinking behavior is to be expected. Hence the call to fun: "Let's party!" For example, at college, excessive drinking can be generally encouraged in alcohol-fueled socializing, and in fraternities or sororities that celebrate pledging and initiations with a lot of drink.

For many young people, it is only toward the end of trial independence, around age twenty-three or so, with more structure and responsibility and maturity in their lives, that impulsive substance use starts to decline and moderate. Until then, the risk of harmful involvement is substantial.

As a parent, you need to be aware of how common substance use is during late adolescence (the high school years.) Some parents don't consider this because they didn't know that their child used substances even before leaving home. But in living apart from family during trial independence, young people are an open market for all kinds of illicit drugs or legal drugs illicitly obtained. So if a smart young person does something really stupid and gets into serious difficulty from poor judgment during trial independence, parents should always consider the possibility that substances were involved. Ask your child: "Had you or other people not been drinking (or taking drugs), would the same choices have been made?"

Whether it is before or after young people boomerang home, parents can help them understand substance use and its consequences by explaining the following:

- "We all live in a drug-filled world, but today there are more legal and illicit psychoactive substances sold and available than ever before."
- "Any drug is just a poison with a purpose—although taken for a beneficial purpose, it always carries the risk of harmful side effects."

- "Taking any recreational drug is always a bet—you hope the reward is worth the risk as you gamble with your own well-being."
- "Because they alter your perception, mood, and judgment, popular psychoactive drugs like alcohol and marijuana can also affect your decision making."
- "If you decide to use, remember that the poison is in the dose, so start low and go slow."
- "Because substances alter judgment, evaluating the effects of use after use has begun is harder to do."

And when it comes to alcohol, the drug that causes the most widespread human harm, parents can share these guidelines for safe drinking:

- "Drink if you freely choose to, not because you feel socially or emotionally pressured to."
- "Drink slowly enough so that you keep your judgment clear."
- "Drink within limits that keep you from causing problems for yourself or others."
- "Find other ways to have fun with people that do not include drinking."
- "Feel free to say when you have had enough and stop there."
- "Don't drink to get drunk."
- "Don't drink to fit in with or keep up with others."
- "Don't drink to medicate unhappiness or insecurity."

- "Don't drink to prove how much you can drink."
- "Don't mix drinking with other drug use."

Freedom is the adolescent drug of choice. Last-stage adolescents want freedom from childhood restraints and for adult behaviors. Substance use is one way for them to achieve a state of freedom in which in the everlasting moment it feels as if nothing were forbidden and everything were permitted. Drugs are not just physically intoxicating; they are psychologically intoxicating. They create an instantaneous sense of limitless possibility for young people, at a time when throwing off and expanding limits is what adolescents most want to do.

But these new freedoms can lead to serious troubles. As a parent, you can listen for trouble signs once your son or daughter has moved away.

RECOGNIZING SIGNS OF TROUBLE WITH SUBSTANCES

For young people who are just entering trial independence, combining alcohol or other drugs with more freedom and impulsivity, and with more loneliness and insecurity away from home, can provide a recipe for problematic substance use.

Take the case of a girl who hadn't gone to many parties in high school and mostly abstained from alcohol, but had been swept up in the party scene when she got to college. (Most colleges do not curb drinking by their underage students.) One nervous night, she drank too much too fast. According to what little she remembered afterward, a resident assistant in the dorm probably saved her life. Hearing her vomit and then seeing the dangerous shape the girl was in, the RA called 911. An ambulance arrived and took her to the hospital, where she was given fluids. Then she was transferred to a detox facility, where she was monitored and kept overnight for observation until her blood alcohol level returned to normal. Hopefully, this was a severe enough wake-up call for the young woman to understand that alcohol can be not only a social lubricant, a stimulant, a depressant, and an intoxicant but also, in sufficient amount, a deadly poison.

On campus or off campus, in school or on the job, the three to five years after high school are a period of extremely heavy and varied use of alcohol and other drugs that disorganizes the lives of many young people. The alcohol- and drug-related problems during this stage are legion.

How largely do substances loom over this age? Think about it this way. There are ten dire risks for adolescents to which parents must be alert:

1. *Social violence*: fights, assaults, victimization
2. *Accidental injury*: mishap from carelessness, impulsiveness, not thinking clearly
3. *Academic failure*: not attending class, not turning in work, missing deadlines
4. *Indebtedness*: gambling, overspending, having unpaid bills
5. *Repeated job loss*: inability to get to work, to do the work, to get along at work

6. *Illegal activities*: theft, fraud, arrests and other lawbreaking
7. *Sexual misadventures*: unsafe sex, rape, sexual disease, pregnancy
8. *Suicidal despondency*: self-mutilation, acts of desperation, attempted self-destruction
9. *Dangerous risk taking*: search for excitement, competitive daring, showing off
10. *Alcohol and other drug abuse*: drunk driving, public intoxication, overdoses

Eliminate the last of the ten risks, and you dramatically reduce the incidence of the other nine. Adolescence is, by definition, a risky process during which young people are eager to try more "worldly" experiences. Substance use only increases those normal risks. A sober path through the last stage of adolescence is the safest of all.

These risks can be elevated for young people who are already taking prescribed psychoactive medication for anxiety, depression, mood swings, distractibility, or impulsivity. For young people who already rely on mood- and mind-altering drugs to cope, emotionally or otherwise it can seem natural to add recreational substance use to the existing mix to improve functioning, lessen discomfort, or increase pleasure. If your child is in this situation, before he or she leaves home, you need to make sure that the prescribing physician has given your child adequate information about the varieties of harm that additional substance use can do. Of course, parents also want to give their adolescent information about their own history with substance use and what their experience has to teach, explain how they currently manage to moderate or abstain from use, and disclose any cautionary tales about how substance use has affected members of the extended family to whose lives the young person can relate.

Any time parents find out that their last-stage adolescent has had a dangerous experience with substances, they need to make sure that a bad experience has taught a good lesson about avoiding such a dangerous experience again. For example, if your son or daughter is arrested for drunk driving, he or she must face all court-decreed consequences, and you must hold him or her responsible for any legal costs, deny him or her use of a car, obtain a qualified assessment of his or her alcohol use, and ensure that he or she follows recommendations for treatment help. These can be times for parents to impose a time-out from college or living away and bring the young people home to get some help assessing the dangers of their substance use. Serious incidents can be a sign, to quote Alcoholics Anonymous, that "life has become unmanageable."

So what are some signs of problem substance use parents can look for? Here are some uncharacteristic changes to look for:

- Smart kids making stupid decisions
- Good kids acting bad
- Truthful kids lying
- Mindful kids being unable to remember
- Conscientious kids becoming indifferent
- Even-tempered kids developing mood swings
- Kids with little money having a lot to spend

- Capable kids failing
- Dedicated kids losing interest
- Communicative kids shutting up
- Open kids becoming secretive
- Nice kids acting mean
- Considerate kids becoming more selfish
- Direct kids becoming more manipulative
- Responsible kids acting irresponsibly
- Reliable kids breaking promises or commitments
- Motivated kids starting not to care
- Careful kids acting careless
- Obedient kids breaking rules and laws
- Focused kids having accidents
- Honest kids stealing
- Healthy kids becoming rundown

None of these changes individually is a guarantee of problem substance use, but over time, a pattern combining a number of these behaviors should be cause for parental concern. When problem substance use brings a young person home, parents should assess that use to determine whether treatment is needed.

GETTING HELP FOR SUBSTANCE ABUSE

If your son or daughter is in college and encounters substance problems, there are sources of student assistance (advisers, the dean's office, a health center, a counseling center) to which he or she can turn. Late-stage adolescents working a full-time job do not have ready access to such help, but they do have one protection—they are more anchored in real-world responsibility. Skip a day of class because you're feeling hung over and you may miss some course content, but skip a day of work and you can lose your job. Having to make a living carries a more sobering weight of reality than does making grades in college. But in either case, young people during trial independence often aren't good judges of whether they have a problem. Thus, it is very important for parents to help them assess a potential problem and get help if needed.

Before they can convince their son or daughter to get help for substance use, parents have to convince themselves that possibly having a substance problem in the family, though painful to admit, is OK. They need to know that it happens in the "best of families" all the time. So there are two counseling steps that are helpful to take. In both cases, finding a certified alcohol and drug counselor is a good place to start. This type of counselor can help determine where on the continuum of use the young person is:

- Experimental and curious
- Recreational or social
- Unintentionally or deliberately excessive
- Self-abusive and causing harm
- Addictive and compulsively driven

The further along this continuum of use, the more problematic the use becomes.

To begin addressing a potential substance abuse problem, first parents can get counseling to assess their concern, help direct their efforts, take care of themselves, and learn how not to make the situation worse. Second, parents can have their son or daughter assessed to see whether substances are disorganizing his or her life significantly enough to warrant professional treatment.

Although convincing parents to seek counseling can be difficult (as they are admitting to a family problem they cannot solve alone), taking the step toward getting treatment can be harder still. Feeling defensive, parents may ask themselves: "What does it say about us to have a child enter treatment?" *The answer is, "That you care enough about your child and your family to get the help you need."*

What is "treatment"? Substance abuse, and particularly substance addiction, can adversely affect all areas of young people's lives:

- *Living within themselves*, by engaging in denial of self-destructive behavior, for example
- *Living with others*, by lying to manipulate loved ones, for example
- *Living with the world*, by breaking rules and laws to achieve illicit freedom, for example

To combat such pervasive and deeply habituated self-destructive behavior is usually more than most parents, even with the aid of counseling, are able to accomplish. They are not up against a problem with a single cause, but one that has many contributing factors:

- *Cultural*: rebellious attitudes toward authority
- *Social*: experiences with substance-using peers
- *Educational*: a learned pattern of destructive habituation
- *Psychological*: negative beliefs about self
- *Genetic*: inherited predisposition to addiction
- *Familial*: hurtful dynamics within the home
- *Physical*: craving, in the case of some addictions

To effectively deal with extreme substance abuse or addiction, a more powerful mode of help is required, and the name given to that help is *treatment*. The purpose of treatment is to provide a group therapeutic program designed to help young people do the following:

- Interrupt their use of substances and get support for abstaining
- Come to honest terms with the personal costs of their abuse or addiction
- Start recovery of a sober, healthy lifestyle free of any need for alcohol or other drugs

Types of treatment vary. The most intensive and expensive is *inpatient* care—in a hospital or residential program. The least intensive and expensive is day or evening *outpatient* care. Somewhere between these two types of treatment strategies are therapeutic communities and halfway houses. Choice of treatment will depend partly on the severity of the young person's need and partly on what parents are able to afford.

Upon what does a successful outcome of treatment most depend? *Probably the most important variable affecting how well a program works is how hard the young person works at the program being offered.*

The advantages of inpatient hospital treatment include the following:

- The collaborative strength of diverse staffing to cope with a complicated problem
- The capacity to safely detoxify a young person and assess any physical damage that substances may have done
- The ability to diagnose other physical and psychological problems that may be contributing to the young person's condition

If medical attention is not required, however, then residential treatment may be a good choice. Inpatient hospital and residential care programs have the following advantages:

- They remove young people from their social world for several weeks of drug-free living.
- They break patients' contact with substance-using peers.
- They simplify patients' lives to allow them to focus on the problem.

- They allow for intensive self-evaluation and honest self-expression in therapeutic groups.
- They provide family counseling to help adjust those relationships back to health.

This last component can be very important, because young people's behavior while abusing substances can seriously strain their relationships with family members. A treatment program that addresses these strains can help restore the family to healthy functioning.

A major advantage of outpatient care is that programs do not remove young people from their social and family worlds while working on recovery; patients remain actively engaged with those daily demands. There is no problem of reentry into social reality, which goes with the return from inpatient care, and young people can bring the challenges of coping with the daily stresses and temptations of normal life into treatment and resolved them there.

With all types of treatment, having realistic expectations is important. Here there is both good news and bad. The good news is that most substance abuse problems can be significantly helped. The bad news is that most problems on the level of substance addiction are more intractable, with a far higher likelihood of *relapse*, or returning to use after having given it up.

For addicted young people, treatment is neither a quick fix nor a sure cure. *No responsible program guarantees an end to addiction.* "Once addicted, always addicted" is the reality that young people must come to accept and understand. For addiction, treatment can be the beginning of a slow, long process of recovery, as young people are given a chance to stop and consider and learn and change their addictive ways. Then, with ongoing support and continuous effort, they can come to live a full and satisfying drug-free life.

When treatment, aftercare, or halfway-house time is over, the question is, Will the chemically dependent young person remain substance-free on his or her own? In too many cases, the answer is no. *Going it alone can risk relapsing to substance use, because the power of old habits and the lure of old companions can prove too strong to resist.* What young people need, to translate treatment into lifelong change, is ongoing support to continue recovery.

Fortunately, that support is widely available at no cost, thanks to Alcoholics Anonymous (AA) and other self-help groups modeled on the AA program, such as Al-Anon (for family members of an alcoholic or drug-addicted family member), Cocaine Anonymous, and Narcotics Anonymous (for other drug use). (To locate any of these groups in your own community or nearby, consult a telephone or Internet directory.)

These self-help groups for various kinds of addictions create a fellowship of people, from all walks of life and with varying years of sobriety, who are trying to live healthy and rewarding drug-free lives *one day at a time.* By studying group literature, attending meetings, following a twelve-step recovery program, and having and being a sponsor, members come to help themselves by helping one another, as everyone learns from the exchange about the ups and downs of recovery. Because addiction is so cunningly self-defeating and psychologically complex, most affected individuals need experienced guidance to recover. The twelve-step group can provide a source of invaluable understanding and support, reinforcing the principles of collaboration to cope with human problems: "None of us is as smart as all of us," or "Times of trouble are no time to walk alone."

The AA program has worked well for many people and has helped them abstain from alcohol and recover a drug-free life by helping them in the following ways:

- Staying *mentally sane*: keeping a realistic perspective
- Staying *responsibly honest*: being truthful to oneself and others
- Staying *emotionally sober*: not making decisions based on fear, resentment, self-pity, or despondency
- Staying *spiritually strong*: nourishing a personal faith to rely on

Al-Anon, a twelve-step recovery program originally for spouses of alcoholics, provides a forum in which parents and other family members can get necessary support and understanding to cope with their substance-addicted child or other family member and to free themselves from four fateful errors:

1. *Trying to control the addiction*—Acting as though one has the power to stop another person's use. Al-Anon teaches family members the importance of letting go of what they can't control.

2. *Enabling the addiction*—Unintentionally encouraging chemically dependent choices. Al-Anon teaches the

importance of not colluding in the problem by believing lies or rescuing the addict from consequences.

3. *Emotional enmeshment with the addict*—Linking one's emotional state to the emotional ups and downs of another person. Al-Anon teaches the importance of emotional detachment and separation of responsibility.

4. *Self-sacrifice for the addict*—Focusing on another person's needs to the extent that one's needs own are neglected. Al-Anon teaches the importance of adequate self-care.

Twelve-step programs do not work for everyone, nor are they the only self-help groups available to provide support. As of this writing, however, Alcoholics Anonymous and other twelve-step programs are the most widely available and time-tested. Which kind of support group should you use? The answer is whichever one works best for you.

What is clear is that if a substance-abusing or addicted young person comes home having created unmanageable circumstances out in the world, parents should insist that to stay in the home, he or she must do the following:

- *Get sober*: no more drinking or drugging
- *Get honest*: no more manipulating and lying
- *Get working*: no more pleas and ploys for money
- *Get help*: attend twelve-step recovery meetings and possibly treatment

As for themselves, parents usually benefit by going to Al-Anon to get the support and understanding they need to provide healthy, nonenabling parenting during what can be a very difficult return.

PARENTING PRESCRIPTION

---

1. Discuss with your child the risks of alcohol and other drug use, and provide guidelines for safe and moderate use.

2. Discuss with your child the warning signs of problem use to watch out for and the other life risks that increase when substance use is added to the mix.

3. Assess problem substance use for possible counseling, outpatient, or inpatient help.

CHAPTER TEN

CHALLENGE #8: INDEBTEDNESS

"If it hadn't been for the online gambling, I might not have gotten in over my head. I did pretty well starting out. It was easy money, at least when I began. Then I lost a few times and began playing and betting more to make up for my losses. It was all on credit cards, so I didn't feel the expense right away. But pretty soon it was more than I could pay. So I got credit cards to pay off my credit cards. Before long the interest was killing me. I tried pawning a few things, but except for some electronics, I didn't have that much to sell. Finally I called my parents. Mom's a lawyer, and she was pretty tough. I could come back home, and they wouldn't charge me any rent. But I have to take the money from my jobs and pay off what I owe. No more gambling. No more credit cards. Then we'll see what happens next."

Money can have many meanings. For older adolescents, it can affirm self-worth, reflect social standing, and contribute to quality of life. Although it may not buy happiness, money can definitely finance a good time. Most of all, money is about freedom, because it gives young people the power to choose to buy what they want to have or do. *Money buys control.*

Money can be given, earned, or borrowed, but any way it comes, there are usually some strings attached. When it's given, there can be expectations attached to what it pays for—as when parents want their daughter to work hard in college for the financial sacrifice they are making to help her attend school. When it's earned, there can be a sense of entitlement for how to spend the money—as when a young person feels he should be able to buy what he likes with the income he makes. When it's borrowed, there is the obligation to the borrower or creditor—as when a young person who takes out a loan or gets a credit card.

Because the last stage of adolescence is such a large step toward independence, there is a natural desire for young people to gain more freedom of monetary choice—to buy what they want, to keep up with friends' spending, to afford a lifestyle that feels more free and grown-up. In most cases, young people do not have sufficient money to meet their increasing material wants and needs, and they often regret the lack. So when the demands of indebtedness chase a young person back home, there are three challenges he or she has often failed to master:

1. Making do with insufficient funds
2. Overspending
3. Easy credit

To help get them back on their own (or to avoid their boomer-anging home in the first place), parents must help their children understand each challenge and how to overcome it.

MAKING DO WITH INSUFFICIENT FUNDS

What is enough to live on? That is the question that troubles many young people when they leave home during trial independence. And it is a hard question to answer partly because of *material deprivation*.

Material deprivation? It can be hard for parents to think of their teenager as materially deprived, given the basic support that they have provided over the years. However, young people's sense of deprivation is usually *relative*. No matter how much they have been given, there is always more to have and more that others have—others whom they may or may not know. And then, of course, there is the market society in which we live that keeps stimulating consumer dissatisfaction by advertising the pleasures and benefits of what is new, different, and better that will improve and enrich our lives.

With the onslaught of advertising, young people growing up in present-day America have much cause to feel discontent. They are constantly sold innovation, constantly told about all they could have, constantly reminded of all they don't have. How are they supposed to stay satisfied? Then taking on a part-time or full-time job, and starting to make more money, only causes them to want more. That's the awareness that comes with starting to earn money: realizing that there is never enough. As one young man observed, "The more I make, the less I have for what I want." Starting a job makes it easy to get swept up in a tide of rising financial expectations.

The matter of money illuminates a painful contradiction in trial independence. At a time when being away from home means more freedom of action, financial limitations can actually make young people less free. As one young man put it, "I have more freedom to do what I want, but less money to do it with."

Of course, much of how young people manage money during trial independence depends on how their parents trained them in money management while they were growing up. In general, from the onset of adolescence (usually around age 9–13), parents need to begin teaching their son or daughter about the practicalities of money. The first step is to diagnose whether their child is by nature and habit a *spender* or a *saver*. The distinction is often telling because it is a rough indicator of self-control.

Temptation, impulse, and the need for immediate gratification often rule a young spender, who needs to outlay money right away. A young saver can often delay gratification and has patience, self-restraint, and the capacity to plan ahead.

When parents have a young person who is by inclination a spender, they need to have him or her practice saving some of what money comes his or her way. This will literally and psychologically mean "money in the bank" as the adolescent learns important self-management: to deny impulse, resist temptation, and set and work toward future goals. Saving teaches self-discipline.

Parents can use the onset of adolescence as an opportunity to teach young people how to manage money at an age when it becomes increasingly important. One way to think of this instruction is by helping young people make a variety of *money connections*. For example:

- *Buying* connects spending money to purchasing something wanted.
- *Earning* connects the making of money to being paid for doing work.
- *Saving* connects holding on to money to accumulating more.
- *Budgeting* connects reserving money to covering anticipated expenses.
- *Donating* connects giving away money to being charitable toward others.
- *Borrowing* connects loaning money to being obligated to repay.
- *Credit* connects spending money now to deferring payment until later.
- *Investing* connects risking money to hoping to make more.
- *Banking* connects securing money to keeping it in a safe place.
- *Gambling* connects betting money to winning against the odds.
- *Bill paying* connects owing money to affording services received.
- *Shopping* connects using money to finding the best deal or bargain price.

- *Financing* connects contracting money to paying agreed-on charges and fees.

Because adolescence is an age when awareness of the power of money increases, it is the time for parents to start helping young people learn these money connections. Young people need to experience what they can do with money and how to responsibly do it. For example, I've known parents who provide allowances to help their early adolescent in middle school learn to wisely spend and save and donate. And I've known parents who help their high school adolescent learn to manage a bank account, budget expenses, earn some of his or her own way, and pay some of his or her own bills.

In my informal observation, those young people who leave home at trial independence having been taught money connections like those listed previously tend to be the most successful in managing this next phase of independence. By learning to responsibly manage money, they have learned to manage themselves in many other responsible ways.

In contrast, there are the free-spending young people whose suffering from insufficient funds and inability to live within their means eventually brings them back home. If a young person didn't learn the right lessons earlier, he or she needs to learn them now to be able to venture out into the world (of spending temptation) again. At this point, parents need to encourage the development of *realistic financial thinking* for this time of life. To do so, they can explain the difference between what the young person may consider a *problem* to be solved and what parents see as a *reality* to be accepted:

- To the young person who complains, "I don't have as much money as some of my friends," parents respond, "That's not a problem; that's a reality of life. You will always know people who have more money than you. You must learn to live with that."
- To the young person who complains, "It's hard to get by on the money I have," parents respond, "That's not a problem; that's a reality of life. You will always have to struggle to live within your means. You must learn to live with that."
- To the young person who complains, "It keeps getting more expensive to live," parents respond, "That's not a problem; that's a reality of life. The costs of living will just keep rising as you grow. You must learn to live with that."

Without a proper understanding of how to think about living with what they deem insufficient funds, late-stage adolescents are doomed to handle the problem in the only way they know how: overspending.

OVERSPENDING

Overspending results from a young person's lack of maturity in decision making when it comes to managing money. By the last stage of adolescence, young people are much more capable of mature decision making than when they were children. What varies, however, is how practiced they are in exercising this capacity. Among other components, maturity at this age involves two skills: *self-restraint* and *responsibility*.

Self-restraint has to do with tolerating the delay and denial of gratification, imposing these restraints on oneself, so that one exercises judgment, overriding what one wants to do by following what one knows is wise to do instead. It takes maturity to say, "I want it, but I can't afford it, so I won't buy it."

Responsibility has to do with seeing the connection between choices made and consequences that follow, with owning those choices, and with dealing with the consequences so that the connection can inform future choice. It takes maturity to say, "I learned my lesson using my food money for the concert, and I won't do that again."

As a young person's brain matures, so does his or her capacity for decision making. The young person develops more responsibility by connecting choice and consequence, owning choices, and facing consequences. Telling oneself, "Not now" (delaying gratification), or outright "No" (denying gratification), can be hard, though, for young people who have not grown up exercising self-restraint and accepting responsibility. Born as immature decision makers, children are driven by emotion, impulse, and the need for immediate gratification. Self-restraint created frustration, but if parents continually indulged the child to relieve that frustration, then his or her tolerance for delay or denial was diminished. Responsibility is not easy for a child to learn, either. Responsibility means accepting blame, but if parents did not hold the child accountable or rescued him or her from consequences, then lessons of responsibility went unlearned.

Young people also develop maturity by learning to *think twice.* This means that, when weighing a decision, first they ask themselves what they *want,* and then they ask themselves what is *wise* or *right* or *likely.* They delay immediate gratification to create time to consult judgment, values, past experience, and possible consequences before deciding what to do. Now judgment, not impulse, is in control.

Continual overspending is usually an impulsive expression of immaturity. It shows a lack of self-restraint and responsibility around money, as the young person satisfies tempting wants at the expense of basic needs or at the cost of future debt.

For example, a young woman rushed out to the mall to buy special clothes for a party, only to end up not having enough money for her monthly rent again. She called her parents on account of this "emergency" need, but this time they refused to "advance" her the expense. What was she going to do? Come back to family and use the time to get her financial house in order? If so, earning, saving, budgeting, and living within her means become conditions that her parents need to set if they agree that she can return home. Parents can make it clear that this is going to be a realistic stay so their daughter can begin to practice living within her means, which means living on a *budget.* What she earns, what she owes, what she spends, and what she saves become prescribed.

Living on a budget is good way to develop maturity, because it requires exercising self-restraint and responsibility when spending becomes a matter of planning and when one keeps the commitment to planning. A lot of times, however, last-stage adolescents and parents view "living on a budget" differently. The adolescent resists budgeting, recognizing that spending constraints represent a loss of freedom. Parents, however, embrace the notion, seeing the budget as a bulwark against overspending. Both views, of course, are correct, but growing up demands giving up, and to become a mature adult, young people must learn to discipline their free-spending ways.

One powerful source of instruction can come from parents who "open up the household books" for their returning adolescent, laying out the budgetary structure they use to restrain their spending and keep it within responsible limits. One mother described the shocked response from her daughter when she did this: "I never thought it cost so much to run our home!" Then the mom gave her daughter a simple spending formula to live by: "What you're able to earn, minus what you have to pay, less how much you want to save, equals how much discretionary money you can afford to spend."

For some parents, opening up the household books to older adolescents is not something they want to do. Like discussing their history of substance use or sexual experience, sharing about the making and managing of money can feel uncomfortable and is often considered too intensely personal and private. At issue is the degree to which parents choose to share their own experiences so they can instruct by experience and example, disclosing some of the hard financial lessons and strategies for living they learned that their son or daughter could benefit from knowing.

The most important thing that parents can give their child is knowledge about who and how they are, and this includes information both about past history and present functioning. Adolescents who grow up with very uncommunicative parents, very private parents, or parents who want to talk only about the child's life often leave their children in a state of unnecessary ignorance. By instead opening up and sharing their experiences, mistakes, and strategies, parents can help their children learn to address overspending issues before (or after) they try to solve them on their own, often with a risky and even troublesome method: credit.

EASY CREDIT

Come trial independence, young people become creditworthy—at least in the eyes of banks, credit card companies, and merchants, who see the potential for unsupervised spending in these attractive customers. Through the mail, through the media, or on the college campus mall, these vendors approach young people with offers that most find hard to refuse.

We live in an economy that trains people to live on *imaginary money*—spending cash that they don't actually have, what we call credit. Most parents have grown up in an economy in which credit has only become simpler to get and trickier to understand over the years. Some parents can even remember when paying cash was the way to go, putting by money in envelopes for categories of anticipated expenses, or when people used credit not to build up debt but mainly to pay off obligations in a timely way to avoid interest and to build up a good credit report. Thus, parents have a lot of personal experience to share with their son or daughter about how easy it is to get into debt and how hard it can be to get out.

The age-old principle of money lending still applies today: time is money. The more time that lapses between the borrowing and the paying back, the more expensive that borrowing becomes, as more interest is charged. From the hard experience that their adolescent lacks, parents understand how credit allows people to buy what they otherwise cannot afford, indebting their future to their present and increasing their cost of living when payments become due.

If a young person is starting college, somewhere in that freshman orientation period will be the opportunity for credit card companies, banks, and even the college (by affinity) to promote special deals and rewards to get these new consumers tied into the credit system as quickly and firmly as possible. In trial independence, young people are invited to join the culture of consumer debt in a host of seductive ways. Retailers use gifts, free offers, discounts, delayed payment schedules, and token rewards to entice young consumers.

What young people don't often understand, though, is that they have just been enticed into a new economy. In a cash economy, the spending question is, How much can you afford *now*? In the credit economy, the spending question is, How much can you afford to defer until *later*? It is much easier to keep track of spending now than it is to keep in mind the mounting obligations that one is putting off until later. Thus, *easy credit causes most young people to start living beyond their means*. Even debit cards are tricky because young people often don't calculate the expense of maintaining an account and the fee attached to each withdrawal.

Because most young people do not receive an education about how to manage spending in an easy-credit system before they depart from their parents' care, many must learn these lessons after the painful fact of charging their way into unmanageable debt. At that point, they experience how late payments can be costly and how nonpayment can be most costly of all. After the fact, many young people discover five harsh realities of credit-card living:

1. If you charge now, you contract to pay later.
2. If you pay too late, you will pay interest and penalties.
3. If you only pay interest, you will never pay off the charges.
4. If you keep charging, your interest obligation will increase.
5. If you don't pay the interest, the credit card companies will proceed against you.

For parents, helping their son or daughter reorganize financially may involve arranging refinancing, consolidating debt, and negotiating repayment. "What we wanted her to understand when she came home," explained one parent, "was how it's easy to get behind, how there is an obligation to repay, and how not to get in this credit fix again. Coming home didn't mean we were going to shelter her from her obligations or provide financial rescue—just a safe place from which she could get a job and start to repay what she owed. She had bought into a two-year health club membership she couldn't keep up, so one of the first things was for her to negotiate an end to that."

One way for parents to explain the challenge of easy credit is the concept of *imaginary money*. Years ago, a local retailer in my town advertised easy credit with this well-crafted come-on: "It doesn't cost money, just a little bit a month." The power of that slogan, and many others like it in the marketplace, was that it emphasized how easy it was to buy, because at the time you didn't need money to buy, only credit, which was supposedly easy to pay off afterward. Such persuasion encourages young people to commit two errors of imagination: to *imagine living beyond their means* and then to *imagine how easy repayment of those charges will be*. In the extreme, they can get into something-for-nothing thinking, treating credit as "free" money. Another name for this act of imagination that easy credit inspires is *wishful thinking*, or wanting to believe what isn't so.

Sometimes, parents accidentally train their adolescents while in high school to engage in this wishful thinking. They will encourage her to believe in *the magic of plastic* by giving the young person one of their credit cards to use for routine expenses like gas, eating out, entertainment, clothing, and school and personal health supplies. The magic that the young people learn from this is that the card can be swiped for purchases without the charges, becoming evident because the bill goes to the parents, who pay it, thus contributing to the illusion that credit cards provide free money.

Thus, when it comes to credit, parents really need to offer that timeworn but valuable piece of advice: "Don't believe everything that you think." They need to encourage realistic thinking by explaining how credit really works, the benefit of convenience it provides, the temptations it offers, and the traps it can create. In most cases I have seen, unmanageable credit indebtedness during trial independence represents a failure of foresight. The young person thinks only about the immediate benefits of borrowing but can't predict the burdens of paying it back. So the job of parents is to help young people picture the whole story of easy credit, from what feels like free money up front to the expensive obligation that follows. The risk of easy credit is living beyond one's means now and, when repayment becomes due, an increased cost of living later on. Thus, one parent advised her returning daughter: "Be careful how much you burden your future to pay for your present." And if your child returns home debt-ridden, you must use the experience to instruct, not to discharge their debts for them.

For impulsive adolescents, focused more on spending now than on repaying later, *loans* can also seem like free money. In addition, wanting something a lot, like a college education, can seem to be worth the price of whatever loan one needs to take. Neither assumption is true.

So if you child is discussing taking out a loan, before you cosign for a loan or before the young person signs on his or her own, it's important for you to help your child shop for the loan and check the reality of repayment by running the numbers.

This is especially true of college financial aid. *A college loan is a ticket to indebtedness after graduation.* And because of interest, what young people repay will be appreciably more than the amount they borrowed. So the question young people should ask themselves is, How big a debt ticket do I want to buy?

To figure this out, they should estimate monthly earnings from the first job they are likely to get, and calculate between 10 percent and 15 percent of take-home earnings they can afford to dedicate to paying off the loan over a certain number of years. In general, when it comes to college loans, the goal is to keep that indebtedness as low as possible. Thus, it may be better to go to a "lesser" college and graduate with lower debt than to go to an elite institution and graduate with a larger obligation. Despite what young people are often told, a "good" college does not guarantee a "good" job any more than holding a college degree automatically leads to employment. Also, young people need to realize that college is not some higher, altruistic service institution; it is a business, an educational business that depends on payments from student customers to survive.

Another potential problem with taking out a lot of college loans is the potential for a *sudden debt crunch*. After graduation, a sudden debt crunch comes, when college loan payments begin but a young person cannot find a job. As one young man described it: "I found no job no matter where I looked, and now my college loan payments are due, over two hundred dollars a month I didn't have, so what else could I do? I move home, get short-term jobs through a temp agency, send out applications, keep hoping for a break, and start paying for the college education that has yet to pay off for me."

In tight economic times, no matter what one's degree of education, a job can be hard to find, and a college loan can be harder to pay off. In such cases, all the skills that come with knowing how to get by on less become very handy—doing without, doing it cheaply, and seeing how little you can manage to live on. In this way, young people can start to learn what their parents already know: that getting by on the living one makes is hard for most people to do.

If debt or finance troubles do send your child home, having him or her convert back to a cash system of operation by "discarding their cards" is usually a good idea. Also, it is often a good time to teach him or her about the hard-to-find fees that are part of subscribing to any ongoing services. Tell your child: The guidelines for recovering and getting back on your feet should be to earn some money; to budget your expenses; to pay as you go; to know what you are paying for; to save what you can; and to start paying back what you owe, the higher-interest obligations first.

Then, when young people have repaid their debt and are ready to move out again, they will do so with the financial knowledge and skills to more responsibly manage spending on their own.

As for building "good credit" in the credit economy in which we all live, parents can explain some of the rules:

- Don't treat credit or loans as "free" money.
- Don't borrow more than you can budget to pay off on time.

- To build good credit, keep your payments up and your indebtedness down.
- The lower your credit score, the higher your cost of borrowing money.
- The higher your credit rating, the lower your interest rates, and the higher the likelihood that you can take out a loan for a major expenditure when you need it.

The credit economy is not a bad system; parents just need to teach their son or daughter how to manage their participation in the system responsibly and well.

PARENTING PRESCRIPTION

1. Recognize and discuss the feelings of material deprivation that often occur when young people leave home to live more independently, and teach your child strategies for getting by on less money.

2. Recognize the temptation of overspending, particularly keeping up with peers, and teach your child the disciplines of planning and self-restraint that are required for living within a budget.

3. Warn your child about the dangers of treating easy credit as "free money," advocate the merits of paying charges on time, and share strategies for financially reorganizing to pay off outstanding debts.

CHAPTER ELEVEN

CHALLENGE #9: STRESS

"So much to do, so much to take care of! All the time I feel nervous, worried about what I may have forgotten, what I'm behind in, and what's ahead. It's hard to sleep—that's why I'm tired all the time. That's why I feel out of control. The pressure won't go away. It wears me down so I'm not feeling well. Headaches, stomachaches, colds that keep hanging on. When you're independent, the demands come from all directions, and they never stop. There are no parents to take care of things. No comforts that you used to take for granted. That's why I'm taking a break. Living back home for a while is a lot simpler than living on my own."

For the older adolescent, the first time away from home and shouldering all the demands of independence can be a lot of responsibility to bear. With the age of much more freedom comes an increase in lifestyle stress.

Excess often becomes the order of the day, as young people vacillate between unhealthy extremes. Too much of one activity (such as spending or socializing) makes them decide to cut back and then do too little; too little rebounds into too much, and round and round the indulgence-deprivation cycle spins. The result can be that young people think in extremes and take extreme measures to regulate their lives, in a frantic struggle for self-control. As one young woman described it: "I can't get it right. First I starved after I binged and then I binged after I starved. I couldn't even control my eating out! The same with exercising. It was either all-out or doing nothing! I was yo-yo living!"

The last stage of adolescence is not a moderate age: young people feel compelled to place extreme demands on themselves. This tyranny of extremes takes many forms and lasts until young people can reconcile and discipline themselves to the notion that *"some" is enough*—that excess is easy, abstinence hard, and moderation hardest of all. Until then, cycling between extremes to gain control causes young people to feel out of control in a number of areas, such as the following:

- Eating
- Exercising
- Spending
- Sleeping
- Working
- Entertainment

- Socializing
- Using substances

In consequence, in this last adolescent passage, many people go through periods of feeling stressed—anxious and exhausted, frustrated and confused, scattered and overwhelmed. It's really hard to organize all these new freedoms and new demands in a sustainable way. And when older adolescents can't, when they come home to regroup and recover, there are usually three challenges that they have yet to master that parents can help them address:

1. Moderating demands
2. Practicing self-maintenance
3. Reducing procrastination

MODERATING DEMANDS

Consider a young college student who was sent home the spring of her freshman year, not so much for failing grades as for failing health. "Mono [mononucleosis] is what the dean's office told us," the parents explained. "Our daughter told us the rest. We had no idea. She said she just took on too much, was worried and stressed out all the time, didn't sleep well or eat right, got rundown so she was feeling tired all the time, with aches and pains that wouldn't go away. She finally ran out of energy and collapsed with exhaustion. That's when she went to the health center; then the dean called us. So now she's home for a few months' rest and recuperation to get her strength back up. We're trying to figure out what to tell her so this doesn't happen again when she goes back."

What might they say? They should tell her about stress—what it is, where it typically comes from, and how to manage life so that stress is an occasional occurrence and not a chronic condition.

Stress education is an important part of life management. It helps prepare older adolescents to cope with the increased and unrelenting daily demands that more independence brings. When a young person comes home during trial independence because the demands of independence felt overwhelming, there is some instruction that parents can helpfully provide.

The experience of too much demand, or what I call "over-demand," is the most common source of stress at this age. Why? Parents can explain it this way. Meeting demands takes energy, and everyone's supply of energy (their potential for doing and action) is *limited*. When the demand exceeds their readily available response energy, people rely on stress to force their system to meet dire circumstances—like staying up all night at college to get a paper done at the last minute.

Stress is a survival response. It forces the human system to generate emergency energy to cope with excessive demand. It helps people meet the challenge or get the job done, but always at a cost. A common example that most young people can relate to is having to juggle the demands of a job and schoolwork. Faced with multiple class assignments due on the same day that one is scheduled to work, the sense of overdemand creates two unsettling questions:

"Can I get it all done?" and "If I can't get it all done, what will happen to me?" These can be scary questions.

Stress is a survival response for coping when overdemand exceeds one's readily available supply of energy, thereby creating a threatening sense of urgency or emergency. This is why the dominant emotion of stress is some level of *anxiety.* Relying on stress allows the young person to meet extreme demands, but at the same time incurs a variety of psychological and physical costs, anxiety being one.

So, in addition to explaining what stress is and where it comes from, it is important for parents to help children see the costs they pay to endure stress. In ascending order of severity, consider four levels of stress that parents and children should be aware of. At each level, stress announces itself in a different way:

1. *Constant fatigue*: "I feel tired all the time"—Fatigue is like a negative mind- and mood-altering drug that causes a person to feel increasingly discouraged and depleted. Ask, "Has stress worn your outlook and motivation down?"

2. *Bodily discomfort*: "I worry and ache all the time"—Always have bodily discomfort medically checked out, but when it coincides with a stressful time, consider the possibility of stress-induced mental and physical suffering. Ask, "Has stress caused you emotional or physical pain?"

3. *Burnout*: "I have stopped caring for what I usually care about"—When what felt important ceases to matter, treat that change as a loss worth attending to. Ask, "Has stress

caused you to stop caring about what you have normally valued and enjoyed?"

4. *Breakdown*: "I can't seem to get myself going anymore"— When ordinary coping feels insurmountable or when nagging illness keeps lingering on, stress can become debilitating. Ask, "Has stress reduced your capacity to function normally?"

The purpose of parents, taking this inventory is to teach their children how to assess their own stress by asking and answering these questions for themselves. Because these levels of stress are frequently cumulative, by the time someone reaches the last stage breakdown, he or she is usually burdened by some degree of fatigue, pain, and burnout. Tell young people that they must constantly monitor their well-being, because the effects of continual stress from overdemand can be *serious*. Also tell them that they shouldn't just ignore signs of stress, pop a pill to medicate away the symptom, or artificially boost energy with chemical stimulation, but they should instead attend to what the warning signs are saying.

Finally, parents should teach young people how to moderate their stress by taking control of the *three gatekeepers to demand*: personal *goals*, *standards*, and *limits*.

- *Personal goals* have to do with *what achievement* the young person wants to accomplish and how soon. This is the problem of *ambition*. Suppose, off at college, a young woman is committed to becoming a social leader in her sorority, working extra hours in part-time employment, and losing substantial weight to look as trim as her sorority sisters do, all in addition to making high grades to compete for an internship. She is creating a very high-demand life for herself, one that has a high likelihood of stress. The question is, How much striving for attainment is enough, and how much is too much?

- *Personal standards* have to do with *the level at which* a young person wants to perform all the time. This can be a problem of *perfection* or *dominance*. If a young man is determined to maintain a 4.0 grade average, to win all competitions, to be the best in everything, and to never make a mistake, then stress is more likely to come his way. The question is, How much effort for excellence and winning is enough, and how much is too much?

- *Personal limits* have to do with the *multiplicity* of demands that a young person wants to undertake at one time and how attentively he or she should respond to the wants of others. This can be a problem of *obligation*. If a young woman believes that she must satisfy all that others desire from her, must not displease or disappoint anyone, and must not turn anyone down, then social relationships can become extremely stressful. The question is, How much effort to satisfy demands from others is enough, and how much is too much?

Each of these three gatekeepers controls a significant source of demands, and hence of stress. The higher young people's goals, standards, and limits are, the more demand they build into their life and the more they risk stress from overdemand.

To reduce this stress, they must moderate demand, and doing so is under their control. The three gatekeepers to demand are not genetically ordained; they are chosen, so they are subject to regulation. Young people who are relentless strivers, driven perfectionists, or compulsive pleasers often find themselves laboring under constant stress and paying the attendant costs. "What I've learned," confessed one young casualty of stress, "is that I can't have it all, I can't excel at it all, and I can't do it all."

This is why, when overstressed young people return home, parents need to help them take personal responsibility for resetting these three gatekeepers of demand in a way that does not require supreme or overwhelming exertion, only an honest effort. Parents can say, "We need to talk with you about setting reasonable goals and standards and limits for yourself, because how much stress you're under partly depends on how demanding you want your life to be." This is how moderation is accomplished.

There is one final choice for young people to consider, and that is uttering a single word that, more than any other, restrains demand: *no*. If young people can't say no to themselves, that means they can't resist the temptation of doing one more thing. If they can't say no to others, that means they can't risk turning others down and possibly incurring their displeasure. People of any age who can't say no are at risk of leading a very stressful, high-demand life. By teaching young people that it is OK to say no, parents can give them one of the most important tools for managing stress in their life.

Another aspect of controlling stress during this time of late-adolescent change, in addition to avoiding cycling between extremes and being willing to moderate demands, is investing in activities that maintain adequate wellness.

PRACTICING SELF-MAINTENANCE

In this last stage of adolescence, many young people simply do not take care of their basic operational health needs. So excited by all the new freedoms more independence brings, and beset by many new demands, they often neglect basic self-care and run themselves down in the process.

The third key to recovery from stress is *maintaining sufficient wellness*. Young people can do this by taking steps to keep their energy (their capacity for doing and action) in healthy supply from one day to the next. However, in urging this, parents often run into an intergenerational value difference that confounds them.

For a young person, it is important to invest energy in what's new, different, more, better, and faster—to get stimulation and create excitement. So partying, spending, staying up late, "burning the candle at both ends," eating on the run, keeping up with the latest fad or fashion, and consuming energy drinks for artificial stimulation all fuel this high-octane lifestyle. The young person's priority is *change* (too much maintenance is boring).

For parents, guiding values tend in the direction of conserving energy by honoring what's old, the same, doing less, accepting good enough, and going slower—to keep oneself renewed and restored. So adequate nutrition, rest, sleep, exercise, contentment, and relaxation are of a higher priority. They want to keep themselves in good working order, in contrast to their son or daughter, who just wants to keep on the go. The parent's priority is *maintenance* (too much change is exhausting).

Of course, the message here is not either all change or all maintenance but achieving a balance between the two. *The goal for continued vitality is to regularly maintain health and to invest in sufficient change to create growth.*

But young people during trial independence do not handle self-maintenance well, and they commonly fall into a stressful lifestyle through one of two ways:

- they invest in the excitement of change at the expense of routine maintenance, or
- they simply neglect the importance of minimal maintenance because it seems so unglamorous and unrewarding.

This difference in energy priorities—between the higher-change and higher-maintenance lifestyles—is not one for parents to argue about with their children. However, parents can encourage a slower pace of living, one that redresses the balance and supports the nourishment of wellness. They can encourage a *health maintenance regimen* for young people to follow to get in the habit of investing in regular self-care. For example, they can help their child get into the daily habit of eating regularly and nutritiously, getting sufficient sleep, moderating substance use, exercising, and engaging in ongoing activities of interest that renew self-esteem and restore well-being. As one parent simply put it to her son: "We want you to get in the habit of taking good care of yourself, and that means consistently maintaining your health is priority number one."

The most debilitating maintenance deficiency that young people suffer during trial independence is lack of adequate sleep. When all-nighters become the rule—whether to complete an assignment, party late, play a computer game, or just watch TV—young people pay a physical and psychological price. Sleep is fundamentally restorative, so if you want to run your body down, then short yourself on sleep. The warning signs of stress will soon announce themselves: *fatigue, physical and psychological complaints, burnout,* and *breakdown.* One of the best ways that parents can explain the seriousness of sleep deprivation is to remind their son or daughter that sleep deprivation is a very common form of torture. So why do they want to torture themselves? And of course, they should beware the stress/sleep cycles: they get insomnia because they can't sleep for worry, and they stress themselves for lack of sleep; or they sleep all the time to escape stress, and encourage more stress by piling up demands.

By helping young people maintain themselves, parents can help them reduce and handle the stress in their life. But parents also need to be aware of another main source of stress: procrastination.

REDUCING PROCRASTINATION

By the end of high school, a common teenage behavior is *procrastination*—the act of putting off chores, schoolwork, college or job applications, or other onerous demands as long as possible. Most people first learn procrastination when they start to resist and delay compliance to adult (particularly parental) authority in early adolescence (age 9–13). Now the practice of putting parents off begins in earnest. Then, with continued application, they allow it to mature into a costly habit in the years that follow, when they confront the need or demand for work. Roughly stated, the adolescent work ethic is this: work as hard as you can to work as little as you have to by putting off what you don't want to do for as long as you can. The shorthand is: work at not working.

To some degree, this attitude remains in play throughout the course of growing up. But it comes into crisis during the final stage of adolescence, when the challenge for young people becomes taking independent charge of their life. The "enemy" to resist when it comes to getting work done is no longer parents; now the young person, not parents, are to blame for dictating terms. With this shift in responsibility, the fight against authority becomes a fight within the young person. So where the rebellious battle cry of the early adolescent against parental authority was "You can't make me!," the rebellious battle cry of the last-stage adolescent against his own authority often becomes "I can't make me!"

A young man put it best when he said, "It's not that I don't know what I should do. I tell myself what I should do all the time. The problem is, either it takes forever to make myself do what I want to do and refuse to do, or I don't get it done at all. Basically, I make lots of promises to myself that I never keep. I can't be trusted that way. The promise is that there will still be time later to do what I say. But I keep running out of later, so when I get there, there's no time left to get it done. Then I'm disappointed, or other people are."

Young people find procrastination costly on two counts. First, they begin relying on stress to get things done. Because procrastination shortens the time available to eventually meet a demand, increasing pressure from a deadline creates stress that enables the procrastinator to get it done. "I have to put it off to pull it off," explained one young woman. "I have to put myself under the gun before I can get to work—even for myself!" Upon graduating from high school, many young people take this habit with them to a job or to college, which makes meeting the demands in those experiences more stressful, too. For example, stoked with stimulants to stay awake, a young person pulls an all-nighter to get a paper done, staggers to class to turn it in, quickly leaves to go and get a good day's sleep, and misses lecture content that he or she will be tested on the following week. This creates conditions for later stress, as one delay begets another. At worst, young people can get into *catastrophic functioning*, or the use of avoidance and delay to purposefully create last-minute, do-or-die crises to motivate the accomplishment of what they must do—be it work or study or some other pressing need.

Second, when the delay causes a missed deadline or opportunity or commitment, the procrastination becomes self-defeating.

What one wanted or promised to do for oneself remains undone. Now frustration, regret, disappointment, and even a sense of failure can follow.

Procrastination is a cunning adversary. It promises false hopes for later accomplishments, which in turn justifies current delay and indulgence in pleasures. So a young man continues playing computer games into the night, believing that he will still have time before the next morning's class to complete the assignment. But then when the morning comes and he has not even started the assignment, he avoids attending class. When procrastination constantly leads to such failures—a deadline missed, a commitment broken—not only is forward motion arrested, but young people also lose self-respect for failing to do what they knew that they needed to do. "I feel helpless over myself!" one young person exclaimed in frustration.

The relationship between procrastination and stress is a complicated one. Procrastination creates stress by increasing time pressure to perform, but that stress then provides the emergency motivation to overcome resistance and get the job done. A dedicated student procrastinator once told me: "The problem with doing work early is that it takes longer because there's no pressure to get it done. But wait until the last minute, and I rush right through it because I have to."

"How do you feel after the crisis?" I asked.

"Blown out," she replied. "But that's just the price I pay. I work best under pressure."

What she really means is this: "I can get to work only when I put myself under pressure from delay."

So parents can objectively describe the five steps for using procrastination as a stress motivator.

1. Delay meeting demands.
2. Create a time urgency or emergency.
3. Face a catastrophic "do or die" deadline.
4. Put off responding to the deadline until the last minute.
5. Rely on the anxiety of stress to overcome resistance to do the work.

For many young people, a confirmed habit of procrastination that they developed by the end of high school can lay a foundation for lifestyle stress that takes hold in trial independence. They seem to have become dependent on stress to get motivated, to get started, to keep going, to get things done, to feel challenged, to feel excited, to feel busy, to feel important, to find meaning, to feel validated by constantly facing too much demand. In all cases of lifestyle stress that I have seen, procrastination is an essential component. The old quote by the cartoonist Walt Kelly best captures this conflicted state: "We have met the enemy and he is us."

How can parents help their son or daughter stop procrastinating, if stopping it is something he or she wants to do? The answer is that they shouldn't recommend cutting it off abruptly. Procrastination is not something young people do simply because they are lazy or something they can change in an instant. It is a long-practiced, embedded habit of behavior. As one young person posted on one of my parenting blogs for *Psychology Today*:

"As a twenty-one-year-old who seems to be going through the 'I can't make me' phase, it's not that I even want to prevent myself from doing things I know are constructive and legitimately would like to do. Even when I'm not doing them, I want to be doing them and know that the best thing for me is to do them. I just proceed to not do them and end up beating myself up over it. I'm not sure if this is normal or pathological, honestly, but I'm nowhere near who I can be and want to be because of it. Consider the possibility of this being the case for your eighteen- to twenty-three-year-old. It may be that they don't even want to be the way they are and want help changing (but may be afraid to speak)."

A young person such as this young man needs help to change his or her ways. The battle against procrastination can feel like a lonely struggle, so help your child see that you are on his or her side in this fight.

Instead of cutting off procrastination altogether, suggest a gradual approach to reducing procrastination. Each time a young person is inclined to procrastinate in the face of some unwanted demand, parents can encourage him or her to start the task a little earlier than planned. Young people don't have to fight the habit. They can still procrastinate but can try doing it a little less by slightly moving back the starting time. In many cases, it is easier to reduce procrastination by doing it less than resolving (and usually failing) to cease procrastinating at once.

As the old habit gradually wears away, young people are able to liberate themselves from painful delay, to enjoy the satisfaction that timely accomplishment brings. Their capacity for independence is restored. *The antidote to procrastination is determination, because when motivation becomes committed and effort is consistent, the engine of accomplishment is hard to stop.*

Stress will come up in everyone's life, but it should not control anyone's life. By helping young people learn to moderate demands, maintain their health and well-being, and reduce procrastination, parents will help them lay the foundation for a *moderately* stressful life.

PARENTING PRESCRIPTION

1. Identify overdemand as the most common source of stress; discuss with your child the warning signs of stress, and present choices for moderating demand by taking responsibility for setting realistic goals, standards, and limits.

2. Help your child develop a regimen of sufficient self-maintenance to keep precious energy in adequate supply to meet daily demands without having to resort to stress.

3. Recognize procrastination as a major source of stress during trial independence, and discuss strategies with your child for moderating this behavior to meet commitments and accomplish work in a timely way.

CHAPTER TWELVE

CHALLENGE #10: EMOTIONAL CRISIS

"It started with feeling frustrated by how hard life had suddenly become. I needed to find my way and make my way and earn my way with no good idea of where I wanted to go. I felt aimless and pointless and I got really down. That's when the anxiety set in, and the partying didn't help. I felt scared all the time, scared of not getting anywhere. And I felt so alone. All these hard feelings were closing in. Then I started holing up in my room, not going out, not going to class, not answering the phone, all the time watching TV, too tired to sleep. It got pretty unhappy. That's when my parents paid a visit, saw how much of a funk I was in, [and] told me to come home and get some counseling to work my way back out. Part of feeling so bad was feeling that there was no way to feel any better."

Trial independence is a very emotionally vulnerable time. Separating from home, moving off on one's own, finding one's footing, managing self-governance, performing one's work, and setting a direction in life are all difficult, and fraught with expectations. Parents expect older adolescents to handle this transition, and young people expect it of themselves. And when they don't or feel they can't, all kinds of negative feelings come into play. *Disappointment* and *frustration with oneself* are often the gateway emotions to more painful ones: discouragement, anxiety, anger, despondency, loneliness, and, at worst, despair.

When a young person comes home in need of recovery from such emotional duress, it's normal for parents not to know exactly how to act—should they act as if everything is okay and be casual as usual, or should they act as if everything is not okay and be careful to tiptoe around? Actually, parents need to balance two kinds of responses. They need to maintain normal expectations, to encourage normal functioning. But they also need to practice sensitivity in response to their child's troubled feelings. This is hard to do. At this juncture, there are three kinds of parental support that can really make a difference:

1. Getting counseling help
2. Separating thinking from feeling
3. Changing the emotional context

GETTING COUNSELING HELP

From what I've seen in counseling, young men and women frequently manage emotions quite differently. Women appear more accustomed to talking about their emotions (more practiced in

being intimate) than men, who are more accustomed to suppress-
ing theirs emotions (more practiced in appearing independent).
In addition, to the degree that men are socialized to believe that
asking for help shows a lack of self-sufficiency and is a sign of
weakness, they can be resistant to seeking help on that score too
(wanting to appear "manly" and "strong").

So when it comes to seeking psychological help for emotional
distress, young women may be more open to counseling than young
men. This may mean that parents will need to give more encouragement to a son to get counseling than to a daughter, who may be
more receptive. But male or female, young people who are open
to counseling—and to improving emotional access and communication along the way—not only gain help during crisis but also
develop skills to deal with periods of emotional upheaval later in life.
I am reminded of the young woman who returned home in a state
of depression, sought psychological help, and in the exit interview
came up with this summary statement at the end: "Periods of
emotional pain are one opportunity to live deeply within myself.
So long as I am in pain, I know that I have much to learn about
myself. So long as I keep learning about myself, my pain will make
me stronger. As I grow stronger, I will be better able to withstand
the hard times in my life."

In general, when young people come home after independence
has failed to take hold, there is a lot of sorting out to do, mostly
through self-reflection. There are also talks with parents, who are
skilled at mentoring and able to safely, supportively, and specifically suggest choices for finding one's way. And then counseling can

provide additional assistance. This help can be very productive at this juncture, because young people are usually motivated to bring clarity to what feels like confusion, order to what feels like chaos, direction to what feels like aimlessness, peace to what feel like irresolvable conflicts, and to gain relief from what feels like inescapable suffering.

What sorts of issues might lead you and your child to consider counseling? Consider some common emotional hard times that young people encounter during trial independence:

- *Depression*: spells of sadness over a loss or failure, over discouragement or disappointment; parents may notice despondency that the young person cannot dispel.
- *Loneliness*: spells of feeling cut off, disconnected, not understood, and alone; parents may notice lack of social companionship and social isolation of the young person.
- *Self-rejection*: spells of not liking and/or valuing the person one is becoming, or of being troubled by a negative self-image; parents may notice how the young person is prone to harsh self-criticism.
- *Anxiety*: spells of acute worry about adequately coping with challenges at hand and in the future; parents may notice how fear prevents the young person from pursuing healthy possibilities.
- *Distractibility*: spells of not being able to concentrate because there is so much to keep track of and consider; parents may notice the young person's inability to stay focused long enough to carry effort to completion.

- *Compulsiveness*: spells of indulging in repetitive behaviors for imposing order to feel safer or more in control; parents may notice the young person's dependence on ritual actions for managing security in life.

- *Escape*: spells of evading responsibilities and commitments; Parents may notice the young person's increasing investment of time and energy in activities that keep him distracted, diverted, and disengaged.

- *Extremism*: spells of all-or-nothing behaviors, often alternating between the two, to achieve emotional balance; parents may notice alterations between excess and deficiency in eating, sleeping, working, exercising, or spending.

- *Aggression*: spells of fighting self and others to gain control over what is happening, often as an expression of fear or frustration; parents may notice that the young person is more quarrelsome or appears angry much of the time.

- *Lability*: spells of dramatically shifting emotional states between feeling up and down; parents may notice unpredictable mood swings between feeling very good and very bad, between high hopes and deep despair.

- *Confusion*: spells of incapacitating indecision; parents may notice the young person's inability to get organized, maintain consistency, or make up his or her mind.

If your child is experiencing any of these, how can you know whether it's a serious issue or just a normal part of growing up? It comes down to whether it's a *spell* or a *condition*. The distinction to make here is that a spell is of short duration and is over, but a condition is ongoing, without an end in sight. Duration makes a difference.

And that is what parents need to help the young person understand. Being unhappy or emotionally troubled some of the time is normal during the last stage of adolescence; being so most of the time is not and needs attention. When negative emotion becomes too *intensive* (too deeply painful, like panic attacks) or too *extensive* (too lasting, like chronic anxiety), parents and young people should seek some psychological assessment, because in either case, the condition is debilitating.

So how do you tell whether it's a spell or a condition? Parents need to evaluate their child's capacity to talk about what is going on, the length of time these feelings last, and the behaviors that they precipitate. Parents should seek some kind of psychological help in the following situations:

- The young person's normal functioning is diminished.
- The young person can't seem to talk about what is going on.
- The difficult emotional state lasts for more than several months.
- The young person is engaging in self-defeating or self-destructive behavior.

Seeking counseling when a young person returns home is usually a good investment of time, energy, and money. This is because the last-stage adolescent is in a time of life in which powerful understanding and meaningful reorganization can emerge. Coming home is not wasted time; it is a useful time to engage in supportive self-examination, to formulate future plans, and to take constructive steps to build a bridge back to independent living. In all three objectives, counseling can help.

Often these days, though, people may choose to use medication first instead of counseling. However, the use of psychoactive medication should be the last choice, not the first. And with the use of medications, psychological counseling should still be in place. Psychoactive medication is a useful palliative. However, although it can help alleviate the symptoms, it yields no self-understanding, and so it generates no capacity for personal growth or change. Just medicating can be a wasted opportunity. Why go through a period of intense, even debilitating, emotional pain during trial independence, dealing with significant mental health issues, and not profit from the experience? Counseling provides the opportunity of getting to know oneself on a deeper level and developing strategies for self-management one did not have before.

So if your child does decide to try counseling, find a counselor (one of the same sex is often best) who is experienced in working with clients or patients of this age, an experienced and trained consultant, unconnected to family, who can provide a constructive, objective, and confidential response.

Counseling is a chance to open up about what is going on, to gain self-understanding, to profit from hard experience, and to develop coping strategies to make it through a hard time. The challenge for parents of young people in counseling is to be supportive of the help without prying into what matters young people are disclosing. It is natural for parents to be curious and concerned, but it is usually best if they do not interfere. Intimacy with the helper requires privacy from parents, so it is best to respect counseling as an act of independence through which the young person is working to get his or her life together.

Giving young people psychological space at home, within limits of responsible conduct in the family, is supportive as well. When tempted to say something about "the problem," parents might want to ask themselves three noninterference questions that I once heard in Al-Anon many years ago:

- "Does it need to be said?"
- "Does it need to be said now?"
- "Does it need to be said by me?"

And remember this: "A laugh is the shortest distance between two people." So parents shouldn't get so serious with their son or daughter that they don't take time to laugh together, to loosen up, to lighten up, to gain perspective, and to keep close. Also keep in mind that how parents emotionally respond to their returning son or daughter influences how their child emotionally responds to him- or herself.

Parents need to ponder a very simple question: "When our child is going through a hard time, even of his or her own making, which response of ours is most helpful—expressing criticism, worry, and pessimism or acceptance, confidence, and optimism?"

In general, a positive parental response is more productive than a negative one, because it influences young people to view themselves in a positive way.

In addition to counseling, parents can help their child manage their unhappiness in a positive way by showing them how to separate thinking from feeling.

SEPARATING THINKING FROM FEELING

When a young person comes home in emotional crisis, parents need to understand the healthy function of emotions. Strange to say, but emotions are too important to act upset about.

Emotions are a powerful source of understanding. Like our capacities to see, hear, smell, touch, intuit, and think, our capacity to *feel* is an important tool for self-awareness. Just as being blind or deaf can be partly disabling, to be out of contact with or cut off from one's emotions can be partly disabling, too. Knowing how one feels is very important to understanding life experience. And your child's access to his or her feelings, and the ability to understand those feelings, are key to recovery. If anything, these crises are a function of emotional overload—painful to experience but rich in what it has to teach.

The primary value of emotions is to inform people of their reaction to a significant life experience and then focus attention on that experience and energize some manner of response. For example, in reaction to some mistreatment, the emotion of anger can empower a young person to make a number of responses:

- *An expressive response*: "I feel mad about what you did."
- *A corrective response*: "Please don't do that again."
- *A protective response*: "Do that again, and I'll report what you did."

Emotions are always worth listening and attending to, because of their informing, focusing, and energizing properties. In one form or another, emotions all say: "Be alert, something important is happening in my life right now, something that merits attending to."

For parents, during these times of emotional upheaval for their child, it helps to affirm the honest value of emotions, accepting feelings without discounting or arguing about them.

Don't do as the parents who took their daughter's complaints about financial anxiety personally did. They reacted as though she were blaming them, as though she had no right to her anxiety because they were providing her adequate support. In fact, what their daughter was describing was her struggle to fit in with her new college friends, who had more spending money than she did. Spending more money than she had to cope with the pressures of keeping up socially, she was constantly worried about living on terms she could not afford and how she would pay back what she had charged. Instead of invalidating their daughter's worries, her parents (and she) would have done better to honor her feelings. Then they could have discussed how to best manage the latest turn of events.

Parents also need to be aware of how we tend to judge emotions. Although feelings are neither good nor bad, people tend to assign them that distinction on the basis of the experience of that emotion. Thus, comfortable, "good" emotions may include pride (focusing on accomplishment), love (focusing on devotion), joy (focusing on fulfillment), interest (focusing on attraction), and gratitude (focusing on appreciation). In general, people are happy to experience these and other positive feelings. Uncomfortable, "bad" emotions, by contrast, may include fear (focusing on danger), pain (focusing on injury), grief (focusing on loss), anger (focusing on violation), and frustration (focusing on blockage). In general, people are unhappy to experience these and other negative feelings.

Now comes the tricky part for the emotionally charged adolescent, a part in which parents have a helpful role to play. Emotions, particularly of the "bad" or unhappy kind, can create a special jeopardy for troubled young people. The reason for this risk is that, *even though emotions are very good informants, they can be very bad advisers.* When older adolescents allow unhappy feelings to "think" for them, what "feels" like the right way to make things better is often exactly what will make things worse. Consider just a few common examples:

- *Depression* can counsel withdrawal instead of engagement to make things better.
- *Apathy* can counsel indifference instead of looking for ways to make things better.
- *Discouragement* can counsel one to look at all the negative instead of looking for the positive to make things better.
- *Anger* can counsel retaliation instead of finding a constructive way to address the wrong to make things better.

- *Fear* can counsel running away instead of standing and facing the threat to make things better.
- *Hopelessness* can counsel one not to act instead of taking charge to make things better.
- *Helplessness* can counsel that there's nothing to be done instead of taking charge to make things better.
- *Loneliness* can counsel isolation instead of reaching out to make things better.
- *Shyness* can counsel silence instead of speaking up to make things better.
- *Shame* can counsel secrecy instead of open disclosure to make things better.

In each of these instances, *the emotional state is allowed to determine the cognitive choice.* And because parents are not always around to help maintain perspective, it is easy for young people to fall into these emotional traps. The young person becomes emotionally driven by this self-defeating resolution: "The worse I feel, the worse I'll let my feelings make me feel."

The trap of letting emotion make decisions may, in fact, be a key part of what drives a young person back home. So part of recovery is getting rational judgment back in charge of decision making. Thus, parents' message to adolescents needs to be this: "Use your feelings to become informed, but use your thinking to decide what is best to do."

Returning home in emotional crisis is a time for the young person, in a safe place, to let one's head, not heart, get back in charge of how best to make decisions and to conduct one's life. So when the discouraged young person says, "I feel like giving up," parents can respond: "I know how you *feel* like acting, but when you take the time to consider the consequences of that decision and what it would get you, what do really *think* would be in your best interests to do?"

CHANGING THE EMOTIONAL CONTEXT

There's a powerful tool that you can use as a parent to help turn around and help heal a late-stage adolescent who is going through emotional distress. And it involves understanding primary interconnections that emotions have.

Emotion does not occur independently. *Feeling* is usually connected to what the person is *thinking* and what the person is *doing*, and this connection is internally consistent. That means that when people feel really happy, they are more often than not thinking positive thoughts and doing something pleasurable, entertaining, or fulfilling. Conversely, when people feel really unhappy, they are more often than not thinking negative thoughts and doing something unpleasant, boring, or dispiriting. In understanding this contextual relationship, parents can suggest ways to bring their child's spirits back up when he or she is feeling down.

For example, suppose a young woman declares how unhappy she is feeling. First, parents can empathize with the unhappiness and then ask for a term that more specifically describes the feeling.

"I'm feeling depressed," she says. Now parents can see whether they can help change her emotional context. They can ask two questions. First, "How would you be thinking differently if you were not feeling depressed?"

After reflecting a moment, she replies: "I'd think about good future possibilities, I'd think about all I've got going for me, I'd think well of myself."

Then parents can ask, "What would you be doing differently if you were not feeling depressed?"

After reflecting a moment, she replies: "I'd get busy, I'd start seeing friends, and I'd get regular exercise."

This is when parents can make a contextual suggestion: "Then why don't you try thinking and acting those positive ways to see if you don't start feeling better? What do you have to lose?"

In this way, they are not trying to deny her unhappiness or even to cheer her up. They are simply giving her a technique to alter the context of her emotion. It's hard to keep feeling unhappy when your thoughts are positive and your activities are enjoyable.

PARENTING PRESCRIPTION

1. Support your child's getting counseling to learn from emotional crisis, and respect his or her privacy in getting that help.

2. Encourage your child to make decisions by thinking and not feeling.

3. Teach your child how to alter his or her emotional context when feeling unhappy.

CHAPTER THIRTEEN

CHALLENGE #11: FEAR OF THE FUTURE

"My parents keep asking what am I planning to do with my life, as though I haven't asked myself that question a million times. They even ask how I'm going to get started. Started at what? All I can see is hard times and a low-end job if I'm lucky. College put real independence off for four years, but now I'm not a student anymore. I know my education was supposed to help me advance myself, but for me, all that preparation just created high expectations. I mean, all these years of time and money invested in going to college. I better get something good after that! So I've come home for a while to sort out what happens next, to figure out what to do, and hopefully to find a way to do it."

When older adolescents take independent leave of family, they complicate their lives—wanting life to be both different and the same as it was when they lived at home. They want to move out but not to cut themselves off. They want to relocate but not to disconnect. They want to have a separate living place but not to give up their place in the family. They want to become more self-reliant but not forsake all dependence on parental support. They want to think about their future as a land of hope and promise, but they see it as a place of uncertainty and struggle. Independence is their future, all right, but at best they now realize how it is a mixed proposition.

As the final stage of adolescence begins, the challenges of young adulthood open up. The greatest challenge is figuring out how to sustain all the demands of their new level of independence.

In the way of this are three psychological obstacles:

1. Future shock
2. Denial of reality
3. Lowered self-esteem

Without the proper tools and guidance, running into any one of these challenges can persuade young people to return home.

FUTURE SHOCK

Adolescents are on a collision course with the future. Few young people are entirely ready when the challenge finally arrives. And their attitude toward the future changes as they move through the stages of adolescence:

- In early adolescence (age 9–13), the future doesn't seem to be within the young person's field of vision. So when parents, worried by drops in school achievement common at this rebellious age, ask, "Don't you understand that grades affect your future?" adolescents truthfully answer no. They are mostly focused on breaking free of old restraints.

- In mid-adolescence (age 13–15), the future seems to be entirely concentrated on *now*. So when parents, impatient that young people are often unable to see beyond the urgent need or want of the moment, ask, "Don't you understand that the future matters more than the present?" adolescents truthfully answer no. They are mostly interested in keeping up and staying current with their friends.

- In late adolescence (age 15–18), the future seems to be about acting older. So when parents, concerned by young people's desire to experiment with acting more grown-up, ask, "Don't you understand that the future is not simply a matter of playing adult?" adolescents truthfully answer no. They are mostly interested in more worldly experience.

- In trial independence (age 18–23), the future starts becoming a significant focus of concern. So when parents, disturbed by acts of immaturity at this advanced age, ask, "Don't you understand that what you do with your future is now entirely up to you?" adolescents truthfully, and ruefully, answer yes. They are mostly interested in surviving the sudden onslaught of new responsibility.

For last-stage adolescents, fear of the future is normal. The term *future shock*, coined by Alvin Toffler for the title of his 1970 book, aptly describes the age of anxiety that begins with trial independence. When older adolescents say, "I never thought independence day would come," they are reflecting a very mixed emotion about the long wait that is finally over and the daunting challenge that has suddenly arrived. So the curse of getting what they have devoutly wished for has come true: they are starting to face life on their own. The future is scary not just for all the unknowns it contains but also because, as one young man put it, "Now I'm supposed to act like an adult. No more age excuses, no one to lean on or blame but myself."

Part of future shock is future pressure. Both the young person and his or her parents have created future possibilities for the adolescent as he or she has grown—plans and hopes and dreams that can become more daunting to face and meet in trial independence. Now the time has come to measure up to these adult examples, goals, and ideals. And now college adds to future pressure. Educational investment of time, energy, and money raises the expectation of an occupational and monetary return. For most young people, trial independence is when they start to discover how they are going to "turn out."

Then there is real-world impact. Leaving home creates larger social awakenings in a young person who is not only less physically sheltered from no longer living at home, but less socially sheltered as well. One innocent college student described the disturbing impact of her freshman year experience and a social problems survey course she took: "I never really knew the world was like this. It's so much rougher and unfair than what I knew in my suburban high school. I've met other students whose life stories are different from any I have heard before. I see more daily hardships around me that I was never forced to notice before. And then in class I'm taught about social problems that have always been there but that I've managed to ignore. And life ahead of me looks so much more complicated and difficult than I ever imagined!"

Future shock at the end of adolescence is really fear of change, the change that independence brings. Change is that process that continually upsets and resets the terms of our existence. However, some changes, like the last stage of adolescence, are more daunting than others. In trial independence, two fears can create significant anxiety about "the future":

1. *Fear of loss of dependency on parents and family*: "Can I manage without the old support?" That is a lot to let go and give up.
2. *Fear of individual responsibility*: "Can I master the new self-sufficiency?" That is a lot to accept and assume.

Because the future is unknown, it can become the repository of many fears, particularly during trial independence. "What will happen if…?" "What will happen when…?" are future questions that can get young people into all kinds of trouble at this anxious age. Like other emotions, fear can be a good informant but a bad adviser, particularly when it encourages decisions that lead to self-defeat.

For example, there is a legion of problems at this age when future fear fosters back-pedaling from grown-up responsibility.

Thus, to avoid a professor's disapproval for not having his presentation ready to give on time, the young man decides to skirt facing the problem by not going to class, thereby making showing up at the next class much more fearful to do, with who knows what penalty to pay. Or there was the young woman who made a serious mistake at her new employment and tried to cover it up with a lie so she wouldn't get in trouble with the manager. When found out, she lost her job. However, in both cases, painful consequences were powerfully instructive. Better to show up unprepared and admit it than to not show up at all. Better to admit incompetence than get caught in dishonesty about what you did or didn't do. So both young people learned lessons about the importance of facing future fear of adult responsibility when it is scary to do.

Responding to fear is very complicated. Exercising courage in the face of fear usually builds self-confidence; succumbing to flight in the face of fear usually reduces self-respect. However, not to avoid or flee certain danger can be foolish, and ignoring the warnings of fear can be self-destructive.

Because the future can be so scary, it takes courage to proceed, and it is tempting to hold back instead. Just consider a few fears of "more" and "less" that the change of being an older adolescent on one's own commonly creates:

- More unprepared to act older
- More alone in the world
- More self-dependent

- More inexperienced
- More prone to mistakes
- More responsible for choices
- More disconnected from home
- More beset by demands
- More worried about the unknown
- Less supported by family
- Less protected by parents
- Less confident in capacity
- Less clear about goals
- Less in control of circumstances
- Fewer excuses to offer
- Less money to live on
- Less structure to rely on
- Less direction for guidance

It feels risky to leave home because it is, and tolerance for this risk varies. The high risk takers have little problem leaving home, but they may invite difficulty with their new freedom by taking dangerous dares. The low risk takers may have a hard time leaving the security of home, but they tend to be conservative when it comes to managing their new latitude of choice. For parents, this means that they should let high risk takers know that they will be held responsible for dealing with the consequences of any reckless decisions. And they need to assure low risk takers that communication with home and family will be as frequent as comfort and the need to remain well connected require.

As a parent, you must do a complicated dance between your child's worries and your own. You have your own transition to make—mentoring instead of managing (see Chapter 1) and not intervening so that young people can learn from the inevitable errors of their ways.

It's hard for parents to hear about mishaps from bad decisions and broken agreements and not want to rush in and do something to extricate their son or daughter, or at least give vent to anxiety about the young person's lack of maturity. But parents who encumber older adolescents with help can enable continued dependency, whereas parents who frighten older adolescents with worry or despair can discourage the risks of independence. It's better to respect resourcefulness and communicate confidence: "You chose your way into this difficulty, and we believe you have what it takes to choose your way out."

It can be hard for parents to be patient with the effects of fear, especially because fear of the future can disable efforts in the present. But should young people express their fears at this age, it's better for parents to empathize and not discredit them. Consider a young man who sits around the house all day, afraid of failure and rejection from job applications, who follows fear's advice to escape those dangers by avoiding applying for jobs at all. Future shock has him frozen with fear. It becomes disabling. Doing nothing feels safer than doing something.

Rather than give way to frustration, how might parents respond to this reluctant applicant? First, they can honor the fear:

"Yes, it's scary, facing the future on your own, finding a job on your own, supporting yourself on your own, making your way on your own. But scary is not impossible; it's just scary because you haven't yet gotten started. Courage in the face of fear builds confidence. Even when you try and fail, you have made an effort that builds momentum. The more you apply, the easier applying becomes, even though you may never really like the process of shopping yourself around."

Then parents can help the young person ask *the four fear questions*:

1. "What dangers is fear warning you of?" (Rejection and failure)
2. "What is fear advising that you do?" (Don't apply)
3. "If you follow fear's advice, what will it get you?" (No job possibilities)
4. "What would you choose to do if you were not feeling afraid?" (Keep applying so I can get some interviews)

Parents can help their child acknowledge fearful answers to each question, in order to move past the future shock and the self-defeating choices it can dictate. The antidote to fear of the future is accepting it as normal, respecting fear's warning, questioning fear's advice, and gathering the courage to act as you would if you were not feeling afraid. Then there is the problem of denial. To not face these truths runs the risk of becoming mired in denial.

DENIAL OF REALITY

One way some young people deal with future shock in trial independence is *denial*. They simply refuse to accept the harsh terms of independence and the stern demands that it imposes. I had one fun-loving young woman describe denial in terms of what she called the "3 P's"—playing, partying, and pretending.

Denial is a form of resisting the unwanted, and it has two functions. First, by refusing to acknowledge painful change, young people resist the new reality as they cling to their old views and ways. Returning home, they lapse into old expectations and habits of having their parents, who don't know what else to do but take care of their needs. The older adolescent exchanges comfort for courage, which frustrates parents who see their son or daughter regressing with instead of growing forward: "She's twenty-two, and she's acting like she's seventeen again, refusing to do for herself, expecting us to do it all!"

A second function of denial is to resist the demands of change by slowing the adjustment down to a manageable rate so that growing up does not feel like it is happening intolerably quickly. Some young people exercise this resistance responsibly. "I've just graduated high school," explained the young man to his worried mother. "I'm not ready to get serious and go to college yet. I want to take a year of so off, get a job, share an apartment with friends, and take some time away from education and relax before the system grabs hold of me and starts to tie me down!"

Then there is the boomerang kid, feeling overwhelmed by future shock, who needs time to get used to this demanding new set of circumstances. In response, parents shouldn't criticize or punish denial. Instead, they can patiently but firmly insist that their child gradually meet the demands of more independence—more work self-sufficiency, more financial self-sufficiency, more household self-sufficiency. And slowly, but incrementally, their child will start assembling the building blocks of independence.

Sometimes, when a young person lives away from home, fear of the future can become so scary it becomes disabling, as it did for the college freshman who retreated into his room and barely came out, his world shrinking until he felt walled in by fear. A roommate reported concern to the resident advisor, who contacted the counseling center, which intervened to literally help the young man "out." At worst, future shock can get a young person frozen with fear.

Denial of the future during trial independence often looks like gambling. Young people partly acknowledge the rules of reality but mostly hope or believe that they can ignore them and escape compliance. They can convince themselves of a wide variety of denial, including some of the following:

- "If I don't use contraception regularly, having sex will probably not lead to pregnancy."
- "If I don't go to all my classes, I probably won't fall that far behind."
- "If I am late for work sometimes, I probably won't lose my job."
- "If I let my bills go past due, they probably won't shut the service off."

- "If I don't pay my parking tickets the city will probably let them go."
- "If I don't do as I promised, they probably won't be angry."
- "If I miss the deadline, I'll probably get another chance."

One young man put it this way: "It's all risk taking anyway, life is. So why not see what I can get away with? Maybe I'll luck out." He was playing with the probabilities. Denial can be the gambler's optimism at work.

This is the kind of thinking that often gets young people into circumstances in which they can no longer support themselves. So parents earnestly explain: "When you bet that basic rules aren't real or don't apply to you, you are gambling with your life, because for most everyone else they mostly do apply."

One parental strategy that usually does not work with denial is arguing against it, because young people, in fear's defense, will usually become more wed to that resistance. What parents can do, however, rather than arguing with denial is explain how it can often make matters worse. They can explain how *denial is the enemy in hiding*:

- Denial is how people hide out from some painful reality or problem.
- Denial is motivated by fear of hardship that admission would bring.
- Denial makes perception of a problem scarier over time.
- Denial ignores problems in the hope that they will go away.

- Denial protects and protracts the problem.
- Denial worsens the problem through delay.
- Denial is self-defeating.

By not arguing against their child's denial but stating how defeating it can be, parents may be able to better help their child move past that denial and start accepting reality instead of resisting it.

And what denial of the future resists more than anything else are the responsibilities that come with independence. That resistance eventually erodes young people's feelings of competence and lowers their self-esteem. Most children who return home as a result of denial face significant self-esteem issues that they must address before they can effectively return to life on their own.

LOWERED SELF-ESTEEM

When the young person confronts the daunting reality of independence and feels overwhelmed and diminished by future shock, a major drop in self-esteem occurs. In counseling, I hear such statements as the following:

- "I'm supposed to manage my life, but I can't."
- "I'm supposed to act older, but I keep messing up."
- "I'm supposed to know what I want to do with my life, but I don't."
- "I'm supposed to be ready for all this responsibility for my life, but I'm not."

Feeling disappointed in themselves and down on themselves, their self-esteem frequently suffers. Thus, it's important for parents to understand enough about self-esteem, how fragile it is, so that they can be supportive of their son or daughter at this difficult time. *To face down normal fears of the future, a young person in trial independence needs the support of strong self-esteem and parents who can help support it as well.*

So what is self-esteem? It is not real in the sense that it can be visually examined, physically touched, or directly observed. Like intelligence or conscience, self-esteem is an abstract psychological concept that describes part of a person's human nature. *Self-esteem* is two words compounded into one. Separate them, and the meaning of the larger term comes clear. *Self* is a *descriptive* concept: by what specific characteristics do I identify who I am? *Esteem* is an *evaluative* concept: how do I judge the value of who I am? Self-esteem has to do with how a person identifies and evaluates his or her definition of self.

Although it is ever present, over the course of anyone's life, self-esteem will fluctuate and vary. A person's self-esteem can rise or fall depending on wellness or illness, success or failure, gain or loss, freshness or fatigue, fortune or adversity, or a host of other changing circumstances and conditions that are a normal part of human experience. For example, an older adolescent leaves for college with self-esteem buoyed by the pride and hope inspired by gaining admission. After getting kicked out, however, for repeated violations at parties of college rules, the young person is burdened by a sense of personal disappointment, defeat, or even social stigma for not "making it" and having to return home. He or she feels like the future has been destroyed, or at least deferred: "Living back at home again just shows I wasn't grown up enough to make it on my own."

At this juncture, parents can help young people learn to take responsibility for recovering the self-esteem that they will need to deal with the inevitable changes and challenges of independence that lay ahead. To do so, parents can attend to how young people *define* and *evaluate* themselves.

Consider the *definition* side of self-esteem first. The concept of self means little until it becomes connected to specific dimensions of a person's life—what he or she does, how he or she is, what he or she has, for example. So being a college student, majoring in a certain subject, and preparing for a certain kind of work provide so much identity that when young people flunk out, the loss causes them to feel as if they have nothing of worth left. Or when a young man, in a two-year romantic relationship with a young woman—with whom he was socially identified and with whom he was planning a future—is suddenly jilted, the loss causes him to feel as if there were nothing left of himself. Or consider a young woman for whom job is everything, who on the way to a promising career is let go as tough times cause the business to downsize. She hasn't just lost a job; she has lost the majority of her valued definition.

"Self" is like a mansion with many rooms of definition in which a young person lives. In general, more rooms of self-definition are better than few. If a young person has only a single room of self-definition, and that room is suddenly taken away or becomes uninhabitable, then the loss of self-esteem can feel devastating. *When future hopes are dashed, fear of the future comes true, and for a time, self-esteem diminishes dramatically.*

As a parent, you should become concerned when your child's self-esteem seems to shrink, when you son or daughter has fewer and fewer "rooms" to live in. The less diversified one's self-definition is, the more risk of damage to self-esteem there is, and the more recovery will rely on building other rooms. In counseling with young people, I see such *esteem collapses* all the time. If friends are everything and a move severs those friendships, if sports are everything and injury ends one's athletic dreams, if career is everything and one loses a job, one must work to reconstruct new bases of definition to support adequate self-esteem. *Low self-esteem can result from a restricted or diminished definition of self.*

Another common blow to self-esteem occurs when returning young people, who feel as though they have failed their future, identify who they are with the problem they have. Painfully preoccupied with the problems that drove them home—homesickness, job loss, lost love, flunking out of college, indebtedness, or whatever—it is easy for young people to fixate on the problem and in the process identify with it to the exclusion of unproblematic parts of their lives. So when a daughter says to her parents, "I'm nothing but a problem, a bunch of problems," the parents need to disagree: "We know it's easy to let problems become the total picture of yourself, but that's not so. Everyone is greater than the sum of whatever problems they have. You also have a lot to be grateful for, a lot going right in your life, a lot of positive parts of yourself to keep going, a lot of potentials to build upon." Then they can specifically describe what those parts and potentials are.

In one case, the young woman, despondent over a broken romance, had chosen to become passive, solitary, and disengaged while dwelling on her painful loss, treating that ended relationship as the repository of everything worthwhile she was—her total definition. To recover her lost self-esteem, she needed to be encouraged to expand and diversify that definition, which is what her parents encouraged: "Get active, start exercising. Start spending some time socializing with old friends. Maybe now is a good time to revise some interests, like making your music." Just as a restricted or diminished definition of self can lower self-esteem, a diversified and expanded definition of self can raise self-esteem.

Now consider the *evaluation* side of self-esteem. Self-evaluation often becomes an issue in response to an experience when impulsive or unwise decision making has led to error, disappointment, or trouble. The following are some evaluative steps that can systematically lower a young person's self-esteem:

- Make a bad choice.
- Suffer hurt feelings.
- Take on a burden of guilt.
- Self-criticize or blame.
- Punish oneself for acting badly.
- Treat this mistreatment as deserved.

So a young man rants to his parents: "I really made a stupid choice when I was drunk. I made a mess of my life! It's all my fault! How could I have done such a dumb thing? I'm never going to show my face with friends again! I really got what was coming to me! My future is done for!"

Although this self-castigation may feel obligatory (he pays penance by punishing himself), it does his self-esteem no favors, driving it down at a time when he needs positive motivation to recover from what occurred. So parents have this to say: "To downgrade yourself when you are already feeling bad about yourself only makes dealing with a hard situation worse. When you are already hurting is not a time to treat yourself badly but to treat yourself well."

This positive, productive approach is crucial for parents to hold firm to during this time in their child's life. If a child is already suffering from low self-esteem, adding criticisms will not do him or her good. Your job is to encourage strong self-esteem, not to weaken it. So when your son, for example, gets back into staying out late with friends and getting up late the next day, and you see this behavior as getting in the way of looking for a job, you need to be *nonevaluative* in expressing your concern. Rather than succumbing to frustration and saying, "This is just the same kind irresponsible behavior that got you in trouble in the first place," you can make a nonjudgmental response instead. You focus not on criticizing conduct or censuring character but on discussing the decisions he is making: "We disagree with the choice you are making about the schedule you are keeping, here is why, and this is what we would like to talk about with you." As when you are feeling frustrated or critical, remember that your child is already feeling far more frustrated and critical of him- or herself than you are, more than you can ever know.

Parents also need to appreciate how a young person's negative self-evaluation can hamper constructive efforts at this point. Their view of themselves affects the possible future they see for themselves. Now young people can be caught in a powerful ambivalence—wanting to commit to a future course of action but at the same time discouraging themselves from doing so. In counseling, these statements of *ambivalence* come in many forms. In each case negative predictions contest positive possibilities:

- "I want to succeed, but I don't want to fail, so maybe I shouldn't try."
- "I want to do my best, but I don't want my best to look average, so maybe I shouldn't try."
- "I want to do well, but I don't want the pressure of higher expectations, so maybe I shouldn't try."
- "I want to be independent, but the demands of responsibility feel overwhelming, so I maybe shouldn't try."
- "I want to care about how I do, but I don't want to be disappointed by caring too much, so maybe I shouldn't try."
- "I want to work hard, but the effort is exhausting, so maybe I shouldn't try."
- "I want to act adult, but it's such a struggle to be grown-up, so maybe I shouldn't try."

- "I want to do my classwork, but I don't want to get a poor grade, so maybe I shouldn't try."
- "I want to get a job, but I hate putting myself out there, so maybe I shouldn't try."
- "I want to set high goals, but not if I can't reach them, so maybe I shouldn't try."
- "I want to matter, but I feel like I don't count, so maybe I shouldn't try."
- "I want to believe in myself, but I don't think I'm worth much, so maybe I shouldn't try."

Ambivalence creates an internal conflict between desire and dread, between should and shouldn't, that young people must overcome if they are to be able to engage with the challenges future independence holds. Young people can't progress if, after every proposal or resolution to do something constructive, they shoot it down as not worthwhile because feeling not worthwhile is how they evaluate themselves.

So how do they overcome the negatives? *It takes making affirmative effort to maintain self-esteem.* This is why, when a young person returns home and lapses into a state of disengagement, parents need to provide encouragement. The intent of parental encouragement is to help give their child the bravery required to take positive action in the face of inertia, to dare risks they fear to take, and to overrule their pessimistic attitude.

One problem with fear is that it focuses on negative possibilities, on the bad that might happen. Fear is infectious in this way. It can influence evaluations, including *beliefs* about oneself, *interpretations* about what happened, and *predictions* about what will happen, in ways that diminish self-esteem and lower confidence in the process. So young people returning home in the wake of what feels like a failure to make it on their own have lost some faith in themselves and have fears for themselves.

- She believes: "I don't have what it takes."
- She interprets what happened: "There's something the matter with me."
- She predicts what will happen: "I won't be able to find a successful way."

Negative evaluations of this nature flow from fear, and they drive down the evaluative side or self-esteem.

The antidote to fear is confidence. Because many young people come home frightened by having lost their footing on their path to the future, their confidence needs building back up. Parents can assist in this process by expressing affirmative beliefs, interpretations, and predictions. *They need to speak up in support of their child's self-esteem:*

- *About beliefs*: "You have the courage to own your mistakes."
- *About interpretations*: "You had to follow the wrong way to find the right way."
- *About predictions*: "You will be wiser and more effective now for the hard lessons you have learned."

It is worth remembering that, for everyone, young and old, the future can be scary at times. So when your young person returns home, this is the time for you as a parent to communicate faith, optimism, and confidence.

PARENTING PRESCRIPTION

1. Accept your child's fear of the future as normal, but discourage letting future shock govern decision making, as that usually hampers future growth.

2. Appreciate your child's use of denial to slow down adjustment to change, but discourage the use of denial to reject the grown-up responsibilities that independence brings.

3. Support your child's self-esteem by encouraging a broad self-definition and kind evaluation of oneself during this challenging time.

CHAPTER FOURTEEN

CONTRACTING FOR RETURN ARRANGEMENTS

"What we learned from having our son come back home after being out on his own was that we—he and us—had to be very clear about everybody's needs and obligations if we were going to make this unanticipated time together work. We each had to know what exactly to expect, and we each had to sacrifice some of what living apart had given us. He had been used to the freedom of living without parents, and we had been used to the freedom of living without children. [Being] back together again meant that we each have had to give some of that independence up."

• • •

"I'm grateful I've got a home to come back to, but it hasn't been easy. I'm used to privacy from living away, used to being able to live my life without them seeing all I do. Now they notice how late I stay out and how late I get up. How disorganized and messy I am. How much I'm on the computer and watch TV. Even how much of their food I eat. We have different schedules and living habits, and it's easy to feel irritated.

I know they don't like some of what they see, and I don't like always being seen."

When one or more of the eleven challenges of trial independence discussed in the previous chapters becomes too overwhelming, boomerang kids return home to regroup. How parents respond to this return can either help or hinder the young person's recovery. Their job is neither simple nor easy.

THE ADJUSTMENT

Returning home during trial independence makes for a complicated family reunion. There are hard adjustments for all concerned to make. Used to freedom and independence from each other, parents and their child have been out of each other's sight and out of each other's way. Back into daily living together, the relationship can feel like overexposure. Privacy is lost, divergent lifestyles must be refit, and conflicting needs must be confronted and resolved. None of this complexity means that family members do not love each other or enjoy each other's company, only that they must get used to living together again. However, the frame of reference they have for doing so is a former relationship—responsible overseeing parents and the overseen adolescent still subject to their supervision—that all thought was over.

It is a natural tendency on both sides to have a *regressive reaction* when living together once again. To some degree, everyone picks up where they left off, back to old parenting and adolescent ways that can cause tension and discomfort. Each feels that the other should have outgrown that offensive behavior. For example, a young person may resume careless household habits that parents found irritating before and hoped would be corrected by now, whereas parents may ask questions about his or her comings and goings that the young person now finds intrusive and inappropriate. Both sides require fresh effort to accommodate each other.

For parents, it was far easier to be blissfully ignorant of young people's challenges during trial independence when they were living away from home. Having the adolescent return is stressful because parents see choices being made that they do not like (such as staying out late with friends or playing hours of computer games) and priorities being followed that they do not agree with (such how their child is spending time and money). And there is usually a difference in urgency. Parents' desire to get the young person's life straightened away as quickly and efficiently as possible does not seem to fit their child's looser timetable. The child wants to take his time to recover; the parent wants him or her to hurry up and get restarted.

At worst, parents can end up riding the roller coaster of young people's ups and downs right along with them. This is easy to do. Because of their concerns and worries, parents may feel impelled to jump in and take charge of young people's choices or to contest decisions that they feel their children shouldn't be making.

But what parents need during this time is a combination of *structural firmness* (about living arrangements) and *emotional detachment* (about letting go of responsibility). They need structural firmness to insist that their child lives on the household terms for returning that they set—contributing certain household help, not monopolizing the computer or TV, and not entertaining friends in his or her room overnight, for example. Parents also need emotional detachment so they can let go and let their child figure out choices for recovering and advancing him- or herself.

What doesn't work well for parents is driving themselves into a state of upset on their child's behalf, then blaming the child for their discomfort. "You worry us so!" No. Parents have to keep a clear separation of responsibility: the child is responsible for his or her conduct, the parents are responsible for their response to that conduct. "We choose how to emotionally react to this turn of events." This is a time for parents to maintain their emotional sobriety, not to lose it, much less blame that loss on the child.

This said, having a last-stage adolescent boomerang home catches most parents off-guard and raises perplexing questions for them to consider. When a last-stage adolescent returns,

- Parents are often taken by surprise: *"We thought we were done!"*
- Parents often feel complicit in their child's unreadiness for independence: *"Where did we go wrong?"*
- Parents usually struggle to define their parenting role and responsibilities at this late stage of the game: *"What do we do now?"*

Parents should not underestimate the magnitude of the

adjustment the return home of a last-stage adolescent requires. This is a major *change*, one that demands at least as much adjustment from the parents as from the young person.

Change occurs in four ways in people's lives: any time they *start* something new, *stop* something old, *increase* the frequency or amount of something in their lives, or *decrease* the frequency or amount of something in their lives. When young people move back home, parents must adjust to all four kinds of change at once. They have to do the following:

- *Start* sharing household space and family resources again
- *Stop* living in ignorance of how the adolescent is conducting his or her life
- *Increase* their sense of responsibility and worry about the adolescent's future
- *Decrease* influence with a young person who is less inclined to accept it

This is a lot of adjustment for parents to make, a lot of energy to spend, and a lot of concern to take on. So understand that, just as the young person has to get reorganized, so do parents.

Through it all, married parents must still pay attention to their relationship. You must beware letting mutual frustration with your child become a source of friction between you and your partner. This occurs when parents disagree about what is best to do, which parent should do what, and who is reacting to the young person in ways that upset the other spouse. Parents must not let differences over the returned adolescent divide the marriage. They need each other's support at this hard time, not ill feelings.

Frustration with an adolescent can sometimes come out as bickering at each other. Parents should understand that the young person's reentry places demands not only on them individually but on their marriage, too. Therefore, parents need to make sufficient time to talk with each other so that they stay on the same parenting page, exchange support and understanding, and work with and not against each other. Their contract for managing this household change needs to be the following: "I'll help deal with what bothers you and you help deal with what bothers me."

In addition, it can help to realize that there is no uniform timetable that fits every late adolescent's schedule of growth. The specific developmental markers for achieving independence vary for everyone, and that is how it should be if young people are going to be able to find and lead an individually fitting path through life for themselves. Because parents have already found and set that path for themselves, they can find themselves being impatient, wanting their child to commit to a course in life when he or she is still searching for a direction to which she can commit. They can feel impatient with the seeming chaos of their older child's life (forgetting the chaos of their own growing up). And if insisting on their own agenda, they can actually discourage their child from using them as mentors, when he or she is in need of this assistance.

Lack of parental acceptance discourages communication. Consider for example what one father told me: "I told my son, no coming home unless he ends his relationship with that woman. We believe she's no good for him, so that's the deal. No change in him, no help from us. We know what's right for our son. And she isn't it. She's nothing but trouble!"

But I disagreed: "No, you don't know what's right for your son. You only know what you *believe* is right for your son based on what you want or don't want for him. But it's his life, not yours. Although it may pain you to watch, only your son can find out what's right for him; and part of that discovery may include learning the hard way what is wrong. So now, because of your criticism and condition, not only will he not come home; he won't talk with you. You have weakened your connection and reduced your influence with him during his time of need."

The dad was outraged. "You mean we should agree with what we believe is wrong for him?"

"No," I answered. "To truly welcome his return home does not demand agreement with the decisions he has made, but it does require acceptance of his right to make them, a right that includes taking responsibility for consequences that follow. If you cannot accept your son's situation, he will not trust and confide in you, or be receptive to what you have to say, and he even won't come home for help. You will be kept at a distance when he needs you close. You will be cut off from communication when he needs your counsel. Your acceptance maintains the connection between you; any degree of rejection will shut it down. Acceptance means respect: you respect his independent right and responsibility to make his own decisions."

"Well, he can't bring her here!" the dad exploded.

"That is your choice," I said. "And with that choice may come his choice not to visit you, either."

As you can see, being accepting during this stage can be quite difficult at times. But as a parent, the most important thing you can do to help young people during this stage is to keep the lines of communication open, so that when your child is willing to talk and in need of your mentoring, you will be able to help guide him or her toward a constructive path.

In addition to appreciating everyone's adjustments and providing parental acceptance, there are three other challenges that the return home will bring, ones you must address as parents to keep the return home a positive and productive time:

1. Clarifying expectations
2. Establishing mutuality
3. Providing constructive discomfort

CLARIFYING EXPECTATIONS

"What happens now when our daughter comes home?" asked two parents who had just found out their boomerang kid would be returning to the nest. Then they answered their own question: "I guess we'll have to wait and see."

But I disagreed:

"Playing wait-and-see when your adolescent comes back to live at home is part of what you need to do, to assess her state of

mind and inclinations when she arrives. This is the sensitive and reactive part. But there's another part you need to do before she gets here, the foresighted and proactive part—figuring out what you need to expect of her during her stay. If all you do is the reactive part, you will end up conducting her return on her terms, and this will not end up working out well for you. You must actively determine what minimal terms you need to have observed. This is where clarifying specific expectations comes in."

The function of expectations is a vital one. They help people move through time (from present to future) and through change (from the same to different), being able to anticipate how the next circumstances are going to be. For example, when it comes to *time*, people need to go to sleep at night with some expectations they can count upon about how the next day will unfold. And when it comes to *change*—making a geographical move, for example—people need to create some expectations about what living in the new location will be like. In both cases, expectations are mental sets that can ease adjustment if they work well or cause considerable emotional upset if they do not.

Without the capacity to create any expectations at all, people can become anxious from ignorance: "I don't know what is going to happen!" Without the capacity to set realistic expectations, people experience emotional upset: "I never thought things would be like this!"

Consider three different kinds of expectations—predictions, ambitions, and conditions—about how the move back home is going to work:

- *Predictions* have to do with what parents and the young person think *will* happen when they are back living together. When predictions come true, people feel in control and secure: "You said you would let us know how late you plan to be home, and you did." When predictions are violated, however, people can feel surprised and anxious: "You never called, so we didn't know if you were all right!"

- *Ambitions* have to do with what parents and the young person *want* to happen. When ambitions are met, people feel satisfied and fulfilled: "We want you to save money from your job for future use, and you do." When ambitions are violated, however, people can feel disappointed and sad: "You spend your money as fast as you make it, so you have no resources to depend upon when you leave!"

- *Conditions* have to do with what parents and young person believe *should* happen. When conditions are met, people feel trustful that rules and obligations are being honored: "We feel that you should make it a priority to pay off your loan, and you do." When conditions are violated, however, people can feel betrayed and angry: "You're not doing what you promised, and now interest from what you owe is piling up!"

So you can see how setting expectations up front can help the time at home work out better for both you and your child. Expectations are mental sets that not only have anticipatory value but also have powerful emotional consequences when they are met and when they are not. So it really behooves parents and returning adolescents to be in accord about what everybody's expectations are, so that they are met more often than not.

What specific expectations might parents want to consider for their son or daughter's return home? Here are a few to consider:

- An important *prediction* to specify is how long the stay at home *will* last—three months, six months, or a year? Set a fixed time frame. Don't leave this open-ended, or else the months may just drag on.

- An important *ambition* to specify is what the young person *wants* to accomplish during this temporary return home. Have him or her tie the stay to specific objectives: "I want get a short-term job, pay off my debts, and complete online courses to get back in school." Don't have him or her leave it vague: "I want time to get my life back together"—or else little else but resolution may be accomplished.

- An important *condition* to specify is which rules for living together the young person *should* follow. Don't let the young person resettle in your home on any terms he or she likes that you do not. Declare what you need—"We need weekend help with the household pickup and cleanup while you are here," "No overnight guests in your room," and "Share the TV and computer around the schedule of use we like to keep." Don't assume that the young person is too old for household rules or automatically knows those rules without being told. Leave them unspecified and you will end up angry a lot of the time, when you are at fault for having neglected to set and ratify your own terms.

When basic expectations about living arrangements, intent, and duration of stay remain unspecified, unnecessary hard feelings and conflict can develop. For example, parents need to eliminate any misunderstanding about financial support. Unless it is specified as one condition of return, it's not the parents' business to insist that their child immediately get some kind of temporary or part-time job. It is their business, however, to make clear what, if any, money they will be providing. It is the young person's independent responsibility to figure out how to generate additional money (a job being the most common way this is done). Most parents expect the return home to be a "working stay." This means that the young person is working to recover from whatever problems he or she brings home, working around the home to contribute to his or her keep, and working at a job to generate self-support.

Another major expectation to clarify is a weekday schedule. Occasionally, returning young people will collapse into the comforts at home—they won't get up, go out, get a job, or get going, just wanting to relapse into being taken care of and to remain in that dependent, purposeless state. For parents with full-time jobs, young people who stay up late and get up late can be a sore point—partly because of the contrast to their own daily labor and partly because they seem to make no progress toward independence. So if parents don't specify and then enforce expectations, they can enable the holding pattern of inaction that young people can fall into and the irritable mood to which parents can fall prey.

In general, it is better to treat the return home as a privilege you are happy to grant, not as a right you are obliged to allow. What young people ultimately decide to do with their life is up to them, but how they live with you back at home is up to you.

Finally, suppose that no matter how you have clarified and insisted on your minimal expectations, your son or daughter simply refuses to abide the conditions you need. Often, this is not simply rebellion against parental rules, but frustration with him- or herself for having had to come back home after moving out; his or her irritation at parents is really a reflection of anger at him- or herself for needing to return. In any case, you must treat the young person's decision not to fit in and go along firmly and with respect. So you say something like this: "We understand by your behavior that it is not possible for you to live according to the limits and demands we set, and you agreed with, for your stay. And we respect that this is so. Therefore, we need to have you make other living arrangements and move out in the next couple of weeks so you can live on your own terms. Of course, we love you and look forward to seeing you as always."

Of course, when living back together, these terms for conducting the relationship don't have to be a one-way street. In fact, a fundamental condition of living together should be the willingness to live on terms of mutuality with each other.

ESTABLISHING MUTUALITY

The last stage of adolescence can be a very self-centered time for young people who, preoccupied with often overwhelming demands of independence, may pay scant attention to the needs of people like their parents. So coming home feels, as one young woman put it, like "coming back to be taken care of again, the way my parents used to do."

This assumption is in need of revision. The natural tendency to revert or regress to the old dependencies, when caretaking was one-sided, with parents doing more for the adolescent than the adolescent did for the parents, is easy to do. However, at this stage, for the stay at home to be most constructive, the parents and the adolescent both need to operate on grown-up terms. This means *terms of mutuality*, living in a two-way relationship that equally considers the well-being of all parties. Such an arrangement not only has value for the relationship between the parents and the young person during the return home, but also has value for the young person in learning how to function in later adult relationships.

So how can you hold your child to mutual account? Mutuality is equal parts reciprocity, sensitivity, and compromise. Consider each part one by one.

Reciprocity has to do with the young person's understanding that his or her needs do not matter most, or more than those of parents. It has to do with understanding that there must be an exchange of benefits in the relationship, such that each party not only derives some benefit from what the other has to offer but also contributes benefits to the other. Thus, parents provide room and board, and in exchange, the young person provides services to help maintain the home. Parents keep commitments to their son or daughter, who keeps his or her commitments to parents. In a mutual relationship, there is a sufficient exchange of benefits for everyone to feel equally like a beneficiary and a contributor.

Sensitivity has to do with the young person's understanding that his or her feelings do not always come first, or before the feelings of parents. It means understanding that, because they know each other so well, all parties need to show consideration for each other's vulnerabilities and special needs. Thus, parents respect the young person's sensitivity to questions about how the job hunt is going by not checking in on the topic every day, and the young person keeps the music down and personal space picked up in response to his or her parents' need for quiet and order. In a mutual relationship, there is a joint concern for each other's comfort and sensibility.

Compromise has to do with the young person's understanding that getting his or her way some of the time is good enough, because parents need to get their way enough of the time, too. It means understanding that it takes some giving in to get along, and that the best way is often a middle way in which both parties agree to get some, not all, of what they want. Thus, parents are willing to live with the young person's later comings and goings at night, and the young person is willing to give parents a time that he or she will be home so they don't get worried. In a mutual relationship, agreements are made and disagreements brokered by crafting decisions that partly satisfy each party, each agreement deemed good enough by both.

These principles of mutuality are not genetically endowed; they are learned through practice. Returning home can be a great time to enhance these skills, skills that will help young people grow stronger adult relationships as they move back out on their own.

Returning home should also be a time that is not as comfortable for young people as living independently was, providing some incentive for them to eventually move out again.

PROVIDING CONSTRUCTIVE DISCOMFORT

Returning home can be an uncomfortable time for a son or daughter. Consider the built-in discomforts of returning home. Young people must do the following:

- Expose their personal life
- Admit lack of self-sufficiency
- Limit social life at home
- Accept parental surveillance
- Be subject to parental requests
- Live within parental tolerances
- Reinstate dependency on their parents
- Experience some reduced freedom to come and go

Yet in some ways, your job as a parent will be to increase these discomforts with the demands you make and the conditions you set. All of this is for the long-term good, as breaking free of those discomforts will eventually help give your child the motivation to give independence another try.

What types of discomforts can you add? You can expect your child to do the following:

- Provide self-support (operating expenses, even token rent)
- Make household contributions
- Operate on terms of mutuality
- Maintain an adult work (or looking-for-work) schedule
- Comply with home rules
- Respect, even help, with younger siblings
- Fit into family routines
- Make preparations for eventual departure

You should not make these demands in a negative way, though. Always communicate expectations is a positive light. Your attitude toward a child's return home is a key ingredient in what happens next. Given the feelings of failure that many young people return home with, parents should definitely *not* treat this turn of events as a "failure to launch." That is a discomfort they do not want to create. Rather, they should treat it as a useful time-out for reflecting on what the first try at independence taught and for figuring out and preparing what to do next.

APPRECIATING THE RETURN HOME

In addition, parents should appreciate the opportunity they are able to provide to their son or daughter, which is not available to all last-stage adolescents—the chance to come home, regroup, recover, and recommit to independence. Consider the young people who have no home to return to because they, their parents, or both are unable or unwilling to let that eventuality occur. In counseling, I hear such adolescents say the following:

- "I have no safe place to go."
- "I have no one willing to take me in."
- "I have no family support to fall back on."
- "I have no parents to help me find my way."

A return home is not only a luxury to have available; it is also a luxury to give. Those young people who are without it are at risk of making bad arrangements for their short-term good, relying on unreliable people and risky situations for survival, making emergency arrangements that make matters worse, and agreeing to conditions that can even be harmful or exploitive.

I believe that when people decide to become parents they have made a lifelong commitment to be there for their son or daughter in four ways:

1. As a source of ongoing interest in their grown child's life
2. As a cheering section to encourage their son or daughter
3. As mentors for coping with life problems when asked

4. As emergency support should dire need arise

That parental commitment extends to their grown son or daughter, letting him or her know that there is always a safe port in a storm, a welcoming place to take him or her back in temporarily when the adversities of life become overwhelming. You need to take the long view. *You must understand that at the end of your child's adolescence, the most serious problems in life are not behind the young person but lie ahead.* So when a grown son or daughter is in serious need, committed parents are always willing to be on call.

PARENTING PRESCRIPTION

1. Clarify expectations about living together so you are in agreement about how this temporary, time-limited stay will work for all concerned.

2. Require a healthy relationship with your returning son or daughter, such that he or she lives with you on two-way, mutual terms.

3. Create conditions of temporary residency that create enough discomfort for the young person to have incentive to move out again.

CHAPTER FIFTEEN

CLAIMING THE GIFTS
OF ADVERSITY

"There were some tough times after I came home, I'll tell you that. I don't mean with my parents. They were great. I mean with myself. I came home running on empty, at least that's how it felt. Out of gas, or at least out of confidence, with no map to the road ahead. It's easy to get down on yourself when you're old enough to act independent but don't know how. At first, all I could see when I looked in the mirror was failure. But after about six months, talking with my parents, talking with a counselor, and talking with myself, I started to see how I had learned some good lessons from bad experiences. And how I had been through some truly rough times and had grown stronger for it. So this is what I think now that I didn't think before: Life isn't meant to be easy. It's meant to be hard. And what I'm meant to do is struggle with those hardships as best I can. And I have. So now, when I look in the mirror, I see a person who I can respect."

Hardship isn't easy. And when an older adolescent returns to live at home after independence has broken down, parents should attend to how the young person responds to this challenging period.

One value of having a son or daughter return home during a time of adversity is that parents can observe how he or she copes with crisis and wrestles with responsibility, restores a motivating attitude, and goes about recovery. Often parents can be of assistance in helping the young person profit from unhappy experience by turning it to good effect.

There are three positive ways in which parents can do this:

1. Treating adversity as opportunity
2. Encouraging acts of resilience
3. Drawing lessons from life crises

TREATING ADVERSITY AS OPPORTUNITY

The other side of adversity is often opportunity. Adversity creates opportunity in two ways.

First, it poses a challenge that creates an opportunity for growth. Numerous are the examples of people facing great personal difficulty and odds who survive and succeed, in the process developing strength of character and determination, becoming that much stronger when the next adversity arrives. And lest young people think these stories apply only to heroic figures, parents can explain that this experience goes for everyone.

Share hard times in your own life when misfortunes, setbacks, and reversals got you down, and how, with resourcefulness and determination, you rose again.

The coaching motto "When the going gets tough, the tough get going" has some truth to it, as does Friedrich Nietzsche's observation "That which doesn't kill us makes us stronger." Lose a job, and the harder job becomes finding another. With that search undertaken and finally accomplished, the young person is stronger for having met the challenge of finding new employment. Experience in making this transition builds a base of confidence for dealing with job loss the next time it occurs, which it probably will.

Second, adversity almost always comes in the form of a change that upsets and resets the terms of one's existence. And change rarely closes one door of possibility without opening others. Freedom from old conditions and constraints creates new freedom one did not have before. Lose a loving relationship, and one is freed to date again. The new job may turn out to offer more potential than the one lost.

Here, too, it can be helpful for parents to recount their own experiences with adversity, describing what happened, how they felt, how they coped, what they learned, and how they came out stronger from what occurred. Life is not a smooth ride for most people. When young people learn about their parents' struggles, they know they are not alone in making mistakes and suffering misfortunes, and they have hope that just as their parents made it through hard times, so shall they. So a mother might confide:

"You know, I met your father on the rebound from being jilted and feeling brokenhearted. It took two years of courting to get my trust back, to dare to trust love again, but as you can see we've done all right."

With courage and tenacity, adversity can turn into advantage. That's the alchemy of change you want to support when your child returns home. Often they feel down or even defeated at first, but after some recovery, young people can leave stronger than before.

ENCOURAGING ACTS OF RESILIENCE

The art of recovery from any misfortune or mistake is called *resilience*—the capacity to rebound from adversity and to try again and carry on. The more resilient a young person is, the more efficiently and effectively he or she can turn one unhappy page of life and proceed more happily to another.

Consider two ways a young person can respond to adversity: *resistance* and *resilience*. Resistant behaviors and beliefs slow adjustment to adversity by avoiding or opposing the challenge. Resilient behaviors and beliefs speed adjustment by grappling with the challenge. Consider the differences this way:

QUALITIES OF RESISTANCE	QUALITIES OF RESILIENCE
Escape	Engagement
Denial	Acceptance
Surrender	Persistence
Blame	Responsibility
Pessimism	Optimism
Fearfulness	Confidence
Defeatism	Determination
Passivity	Initiation
Helplessness	Resourcefulness
Despair	Hope

Parents need to treat a return home as a chance to rebound from adversity and strengthen the young person's capacity to cope with future adversities in life to come. To that end, you need to respond to both resistant and resilient qualities that your child expresses, but in different ways.

When you hear expressions of resistance—like "What's the point of trying?" "Things are never going to work out!" and "I give up!"—you need to listen and empathize, not dispute or criticize. Responding with negative expressions—like "You'll never get anywhere talking that way!" "What a lousy attitude!" and "Giving up is giving in to failure!"—only puts the young person on the defensive, adds more negativity to the mix of unhappy thinking, and drives him or her further into resistant thinking and acting.

It is better to accept resistance and listen empathetically: "I know how hard it must be and how discouraged you must feel; tell me more about it." Responding in this way expresses interest and creates an influential connection that you can build on. You can suggest the benefits of moving to a more resilient position: "Suppose you were feeling confident and optimistic; how would you behave? If differently, why not give those actions a try? For example, rather than give up because you didn't get what you wanted most of all, you could think about the next best thing you want and go after that."

Resilience comes in two forms, and both are important. There is *reactive resilience*, which deals with the past and accepts what occurred, assumes some share of responsibility, and makes one able to learn from mistakes. And there is *proactive resilience*, which prepares for the future and plans next steps, gets help as needed, and expects conditions to improve.

When you see signs of resilience, you need to recognize and encourage those actions and attitudes: "Good for you for being persistent, so resourceful, and so positive. That's how you keep yourself in forward motion!" Should your son or daughter proceed to beat up on themselves for choosing unwisely or for life going badly, equating a bad situation with being a bad person and punishing him- or herself accordingly, you should argue against this: "To hurt yourself when you are already hurting only makes the hurt worse. When you're hurting is a time to treat yourself not badly but well. That way you can motivate yourself to do better."

As a parent, you should also be on the watch for a significant variable that can erode resilience: the pattern of sleep the young person brings home. Used to burning the candle at both ends on their own or with friends at college, young people often sacrifice sleep for the sake of pleasure and the demands of work or study. "I don't have time for sleep," one young man explained. "I'm too busy." As mentioned in Chapter 9 on stress, almost nothing erodes resilience like sleep deprivation. It runs down the human system with fatigue, reduces available energy, discourages a positive focus, and makes minor ills more common and major ills more difficult to recover from. Thus, one of the best conditions parents can attach to a return home is that their child commit to a healthy regimen of sufficient sleep. Lack of adequate sleep diminishes resilience.

DRAWING LESSONS FROM LIFE CRISES

All the eleven life challenges discussed in this book that can come to crisis in trial independence have much to teach. When a young person comes home, parents can play a helpful role in that education, providing they do so in helpful, not hurtful, ways.

To avoid unnecessary hurt, parents must understand that with any form of learning, there are risks involved. What are the risks of learning during this stage? To learn from hard experience requires:

- *Having to confess ignorance*: "I didn't know."
- *Having to admit mistakes*: "I made a poor decision."

- *Having to feel stupid*: "I should have known better."
- *Having to look foolish*: "Others will see how I messed up."
- *Having to feel evaluated*: "I really failed to do as I should."

Understanding how this jeopardy works, you must respond to your child in ways that reduce and do not elevate those risks. At a time when a son's or daughter's self-esteem is fragile, parents must make the risks of learning safe.

It takes self-esteem to learn. The lower a young person's self-esteem is, the more fearful the risks of learning can feel, and the greater is the temptation to deny what the experience can teach. So if young people return home really down on themselves for mismanaging some part of their independence, they may not feel immediately able to learn from the errors of their ways. They may say: "I don't know why it happened!" "It wasn't my fault!" "Other people are to blame!" or "I don't want to talk about it!"

At this point, if you become impatient and critical and try to force the education, you will only reduce your child's willingness to learn from experience. Here are some examples of how parents knowingly or unknowingly discourage or criticize young people during this time:

- *Criticizing ignorance*: "How could you not know that?"
- *Being intolerant of mistakes*: "You weren't even thinking!"
- *Criticizing stupidity*: "Dumb choices are all you make!"
- *Deriding foolishness*: "You've really embarrassed yourself!"
- *Evaluating severely*: "You've messed up your life for good!"

For parents to encourage learning from experience, they must do what they can to reduce the risks of learning so the lessons from hard experience can instruct. For example, parents can do the following:

- *Accept ignorance*: "Education starts when we admit what we don't or didn't know."
- *Be tolerant of mistakes*: "A lot of learning in life comes after decisions we wish we hadn't made."
- *Moderate feelings of stupidity*: "It's not stupid not to know it all, it's human."
- *Empathize with appearing foolish*: "It's hard to show the world that we didn't know any better."
- *Give positive evaluation*: "You're wiser now than you were before."

Parents who punish a young person for not being able to manage all of independence the first time out may instill a fear of messing up. This fear can inhibit their child's willingness to risk learning later on and to learn from mistakes when they occur. This would be unfortunate, as challenges provide great lessons when approached in the right way. Consider the life lessons that the eleven challenges of trial independence have to teach:

1. *Missing home and family* teaches young people to live apart and alone but still remain connected by staying in touch, and to develop independent relationships of their own.

2. *Managing increased freedom* teaches acceptance of the fact that freedom isn't free, because all choices come with consequences, some good and some bad.

3. *Unemployment* teaches young people that there is no social promise of employment or job security and what it takes to find another job.

4. *Flunking out of college* teaches that it's easier to start college than to finish it and that self-discipline is what it takes to graduate.

5. *Roommate problems* teach the complexity of managing a domestic partnership and how all parties share responsibility for making it work.

6. *A broken romantic relationship* teaches that love is risky, that it is not guaranteed to last forever, and that a broken heart can be mended.

7. *Substance use* can teach that alcohol and other drugs that cause good feelings may cause bad decisions, as well as a reliance that is hard to shake.

8. *Indebtedness* teaches the work it takes to repay what is owed and how to live within one's means.

9. *Stress* teaches the physical and psychological costs of constant overdemand and how to moderate that demand to keep the pressure down.

10. *Emotional crises* teach how to experience life deeply without allowing feelings to dictate thoughts and actions that worsen emotional pain.

11. *Fear of the future* teaches young people to brave the unknown and make their way through uncertainty as they chart and chance their course through life.

If you approach each challenge with a positive outlook, giving supportive responses that encourage learning, any life crisis can provide invaluable lessons to your child for creating an even better life in the future.

PARENTING PRESCRIPTION

1. Help your son or daughter seize the unexpected opportunities that came with whatever adversity caused his or her return to home.

2. Empathize with your child's resistance to recovery and encourage expressions and acts of resilience.

3. Support learning from hard experience by giving encouraging responses that make learning significant life lessons from inevitable mistakes safe to do.

CHAPTER SIXTEEN

THE END OF ADOLESCENCE

"It's a scary feeling, starting off on my own—making a life for myself without any map for getting it done. Knowing that what I make of my life depends so much on me. Living up to that responsibility. I'm not a kid any more, free to play around. Good-bye to those good times and not-so-good times! Times when my parents and I didn't get along. They wouldn't leave me alone and I couldn't leave to be left alone. We were stuck with each other. Then I finally moved out, only to move back in after a year, then out again once I got some mistakes straightened out, at last able to barely make it. Living at home is history now. They don't try to run my life anymore and I don't run to them for help. Our relationship is different now. We're all adults now, person to person, equals that way, even though I'm still their child. They just love me and cheer me on, and I'm appreciative of them. Last time we got together, my mom said, 'We sure have been through a lot together!' My dad laughed at the truth of that. And I did, too."

When an older adolescent moves back home to live with parents after some adversity, this creates a great opportunity for all concerned—to pull together and strengthen their relationship during a time that can be hard. Then while your son or daughter is working to regroup and move on, you also have your share of work to do—to anticipate further changes in your parenting after adolescence is done. This final chapter suggests some helpful, albeit difficult, shifts in parenting that can happen next.

First, parents need to understand one thing about parenting: it never stops. As the great baseball poet Yogi Berra said: "It ain't over till it's over." Once you become a parent, you remain a parent for the rest of your life. So the end of your child's adolescence is not the end of parenting; it is only a transition point. But when adolescence is over, what comes next? And then, how does parenting change?

The last stage of adolescence, what I call trial independence, ends in the early to mid-twenties, when young people become psychologically, socially, and economically independent:

- *Psychologically*, there is an authentic sense of individual identity—arriving at a fitting definition of themselves for themselves, and not for parents.
- *Socially*, there is a sense of autonomy—determination to set their own agenda and follow their own path as they make their way in the world.
- *Economically*, there is financial self-support—commitment to earn their own way and pay their own way without the need for parental assistance.

When adolescence is over, young adulthood begins. Roughly spanning the early twenties to about the age of thirty, this period ends when the young person becomes anchored in adulthood in at least three ways.

1. He or she has played with enough older freedom to want to settle down.
2. There is an emerging sense of occupational or career future to work for.
3. There is the desire to find a committed partner with whom to share the journey through adulthood.

Over the course of this progression from childhood through adolescence to young adulthood, the relationship between parent and child keeps changing. And at the end, parents must come to terms with the journey taken, the outcome reached, and how to adjust to having an adult child in their life. In the process, parents must accept how they are evaluated in the their child's eyes, resolve any disappointment or guilt they feel, and understand some of the new constraints that govern their relationship with an adult child. Thus, there are three challenges that parents must meet during this time:

1. Adolescent evaluation of parents
2. Disappointment and guilt of parents
3. Relating to the adult child

EVALUATION OF PARENTS

Children observe their parents more closely, appraise their parents more carefully, and know their parents better than parents do the child. This may seems surprising, but it is true. It comes naturally from the fact that, as the child grows to adulthood, the parent is the one in charge.

When someone has more power than you do in a relationship, for your own survival, you tend to scrutinize that person in greater detail to get whatever edge of understanding and influence you can to indirectly manage (or manipulate) the other person. So in organizations, the subordinate knows the superior better; in peer groups, the follower knows the leader better; in society, the minority knows the majority better; in families, the abused knows the abuser better; in prisons, the captive knows the jailer better; and so on.

Parents vastly underestimate how deeply known and constantly evaluated they are by their child. In the vanity of their superior position, parents prefer to think that they know the child best and are the best judge. And perhaps this is for the best. Otherwise, being the object of such keen and relentless observation might make parents too self-conscious for their own comfort. But regardless of the perspective, it is the parent who is under the greater scrutiny and evaluation of the child.

From childhood to adolescence to young adulthood, however, the judgmental thrust of this evaluation tends to change. The child tends to idealize the parents, the adolescent tends to criticize the parents, and the young adult tends to reconcile him- or herself with the parenting received. Here's how this often works.

The child (up to age 8–9) admires, even worships, parents for what they can do and for the power of approval that they possess. The child wants to relate on parental terms, enjoy parental companionship, and imitate the parents where possible. The child wants to be like and to be liked by these adults, whom he or she mostly positively evaluates (assuming that they are not damaging or dangerous to live with). A child identifies with parents because they provide the primary models to follow and to live up to. So childhood evaluation of parents begins with idealization. At the outset, parents are usually too good to be true in a child's eyes.

Then comes adolescence (beginning around age 9–13), when parents are kicked off the worshipful pedestal that the child created. Where before parents could do no wrong, come adolescence it seems they can do no right. What causes this sudden fall from grace? Have parents changed? No, but the child has, and with cause. To begin the separation from childhood (and from parents and family) that starts adolescence, the young person has to reject some of the old role and lifestyle that branded him or her as child, to free up growing room for the journey to independence ahead. Through attitude and actions, the young person is saying, "I no longer want to be defined and treated as a child anymore."

To this end, part of adolescence is about letting the "bad child" out. *Bad* doesn't mean evil, immoral, or illegal; it simply means more abrasive to live with—becoming more critical, dissatisfied, argumentative, passively resistant, moody, distant, and noncompliant. This transformation, however, cannot be accomplished without a negative change in the reputation of parents as well. Like it or not, parents who have grown accustomed to being perceived as having a positive role by the adoring child must now accept being cast in a more negative one by the faultfinding adolescent. The early adolescent particularly needs to have "bad" parents to justify letting his or her "bad" child out: "Well it's not just me who's become hard to live with, you have too!"

And in this stage, parental company in public becomes more problematic. To be seen in parents' presence by friends diminishes adolescents' sense of social independence. And parents' habits and characteristics can be personally embarrassing to them: "Do you always have to dress that way?" So adolescent evaluation becomes more critical of parents and, with increased conflicts over freedom, remains that way through the rest of adolescence, partly to justify the independence from parents being sought. After all, if parents weren't considered difficult to live with, why ever leave?

Then, in the early to mid-twenties, adolescence ends and young adulthood begins, bringing with it a period of self-evaluation for the young person that soon implicates parents. The young adult question is simply this: "Why did I turn out the way I am?" In answering this question, the young person looks back over personal history and begins to identify significant events and particularly influential people that shaped his or her development. This is where parents come into close focus. By commission and omission, how did parents contribute to the young person's growth?

The answer is "Both positively and negatively." No matter how well-intentioned, the best parents can ever provide is a mix of strength and frailty, wisdom and stupidity, consideration and selfishness, good choices and bad. At stake for the young person is coming to accept having imperfect parents who provided not just help growing up but also hurt and hindrance. The purpose of this reflective process is to come up with an adult perspective of parents that the adult child can honestly live with—creating an understanding and acceptance, as one young person put it, "of my parents, warts and all."

The hardest part of this process, both for young people and for parents, is the beginning. This is because before they can claim positive parental influence, young people must acknowledge the negative influence, and this requires some rationalization. They have to construct an understanding that realistically encompasses the mix of positive and negative influences that parents provided.

In counseling, a young person described the early part of her parental evaluation this way: "My parents sure weren't perfect. Love me as they did, they made a lot of mistakes. Caught up in themselves, they weren't always there for me when I needed. And they made some decisions, like divorce, which really hurt and have had lasting effects."

During the negative acknowledgment phase of this evaluation, it is not uncommon for young people to pull away and reduce communication with their parents, in order to evaluate the painful history. They then resume contact when the positive evaluation is at last put in place, and they can now acknowledge the significant contributions that parents made. So after some counseling sessions down the road, the young woman concluded: "But you know, they worked hard to take care of me, hung in there with me when the going got tough, shared some good times worth remembering, and I know they tried their best."

The negative phase of young adult evaluation can be scary for parents, especially when contact and communication fall away. But if you can be understanding and patient, and hold yourself in loving readiness, your child's evaluation usually leads to reconciliation, and the return to a meaningful adult relationship carries on.

In my book *The Connected Father*, I wrote about one such reconciliation:

"A father at a workshop of mine many years ago explained it this way: 'One rose at a time,' he called it. 'She was about twenty-three, our daughter, when without explanation, she cut off all communication with us. Stopped coming to see us. Rarely answered our phone calls, and when she did abruptly told us that she'd call us when she felt like talking, and to please not call her. At first we felt really hurt, then really angry. What had we done to deserve such treatment? Then my wife said something really important: 'Suppose this isn't something painful she's doing against us; suppose it's something painful she needs to be doing for her.' So that's what we decided it was. And to let her know we loved her and were thinking about her, every week I sent her a single red rose with a card that read: 'We love you.' And I did this for about seven

months until one day she called, said she wanted to come over and see us, and she did, and we've been lovingly back together ever since. Of course I asked her about the roses, curious to know what she did with them. 'At first,' she said, 'I threw them away. Then I gave them away to friends. And finally I started keeping them, signs that you were keeping me in your heart, one rose at a time.'"

In truth, know that when it comes to how adult children finally evaluate parenting, parents were never as wonderful as their child wanted to believe or as lacking as their adolescent frequently complained they were. Mostly parents turn out performing about as well as one young adult, after some hard reflection, suggested: "My parents weren't perfect, but I've decided that's OK. After all, I wasn't perfect either."

If your child chooses to share with you his or her assessment of your parenting, you are not obliged to agree with it, but you should not defend or argue against it or try to correct it. Instead, knowing that your grown child honestly feels the evaluation, you should empathetically listen and accept what he or she feels was true The rule is this: if you want your grown son or daughter to affirm the positive influence you provided, you must first be willing to acknowledge that, at least in his or her eyes, there was some negative influence as well.

It is not just the child who must evaluate parenting during this time, though. Most parents have some unfinished business within themselves that they need to close out to become open to a healthy relationship with their adult child.

DISAPPOINTMENT AND GUILT OF PARENTS

Two great emotional burdens that parents often carry into a son's or daughter's adulthood are *disappointment* (the problem of parental investment) and *guilt* (the problem of parental implication). Both can severely affect the relationship with their adult child.

Let's begin with the issue of disappointment. Parenting is a process of investment. Parents invest not only their care, energy, and resources in their child but also their assumptions, ambitions, hopes, and even dreams about how this person will turn out when grown up. The more investment parents make, the more invested they feel, and the more they cherish the notion of a deserving return. An extreme investment is often made by parents of an only child, sometimes with an extreme expectation of return. "We worked so hard and sacrificed so much for her, the least she can do is give us some of what we hoped for back!" one couple complained after their daughter had strayed from the path in life they had chosen for her. They were treating their daughter as if she were supposed to fulfill whatever promise they thought she owed them.

So what happens when parents, who assumed their adolescent would pursue a conservative lifestyle similar to their own, hear that their child is moving into a commune-like house with other young people committed to living an alternative lifestyle? Or what happens when parents, whose ambition was for the adolescent to go to college, have a son who decides after high school to scrape together a living making a go of it as a musician? Or what happens when parents, who hoped their children would choose to return to their home city after college and live close by, have a son or daughter who decides to move much further away? Or what happens when parents, whose dream for their adolescent included launching a career and remaining single until it was established, have a daughter who gets pregnant, gets married, and gives up the profession they were wishing she'd pursue?

"Of course, we're disappointed," one set of parents told me in counseling. "This is not what we planned for a child of our own! And we told her so."

"And how did she respond when you told her that?" I asked.

They replied: "She acted really hurt, like we had let her down, when the reverse was true! And she hasn't talked much to us since."

Then I suggested that if they wanted a close and loving relationship with their adult daughter, they needed to ask themselves whether their daughter was supposed to fit their expectations, or whether their expectations were supposed to fit their daughter? Their answer makes a profound difference. If they believe she should live up to their expectations and she is not doing so, they will feel disappointed, and communicating that disappointment to her will, to some degree, alienate the relationship. If, however, they believe that for the sake of acceptance they must adjust their expectations to fit the path and lifestyle their daughter has independently chosen to follow, then they will affirm that relationship.

It can be hard for parents to remember that when a grown son or daughter disappoints their expectations, it is their expectations, and not the child's conduct, that is to blame. The parents have chosen to hold a set of expectations that do not fit the choices their adult child is making. When the child and adolescent lived dependently on their care, part of living on the parents' terms was meeting their expectations. But once grown into a young adult, a son or daughter is living on *independent* terms. Now, for the sake of enjoying an ongoing relationship, parents must adjust their expectations in recognition that the life they gave their child, and how he or she chooses to lead it, belongs to the child, not to them. *The grown child is not in this world to live up to parental expectations; the parents are in this world to accept how the grown child chooses to live her adult life.*

What can help parents adjust their expectations to fit the emerging life of the adult child is to ask questions about changes they did not expect, asking help to understand what they were not prepared for. By doing so, they will come to appreciate the richness of the growing differences between themselves and their grown child, and the young adult will also come to value parents' interest and effort in return.

The other big emotional burden parents carry during this time is guilt. Just as parental investment can lead to problems of disappointment when expectations are not met, parental implication can lead to problems of guilt when parents hold themselves accountable for personal hardships that the young person carries into adult life. So a child of divorce keeps bolting from romantic relationships for fear of a partner's breaking commitment the way his or her parents did. Or the young person runs into problems with substance abuse just like a parent, who finally got sober and found recovery.

It's easy for parents to feel implicated in their grown child's travails when they believe that there is a connection between their past conduct and the adult child's present behavior. The more deeply implicated the parents feel, the more susceptible to guilt they tend to be.

Most parents have some guilt about something they did or didn't do that caused temporary or lasting hurt for the son or daughter, some acts of commission or omission for which they blame themselves:

- "If only I had been stricter, my child would not have run so wild, given up on school, and had such a hard time getting a good-paying job."
- "If only I hadn't been so strict, my child would not have rebelled into so much trouble, running with the wrong crowd, and ending up with jail time on her record."
- "If only I hadn't been so involved in my career, my child wouldn't be so starved for attention, looking for it in one bad relationship after another."

The potential for parental guilt is endless.

Does guilt serve any good? Well, in one sense, the parents are not totally removing themselves from assuming responsibility for their own behavior in relation to their child. After all, whether a parent hugs or hits, loves or resents, approves or abuses, nurtures or abandons a son or daughter can make a formative difference. The child who is hit, resented, abused, and abandoned is likely to have a less trustful response to parents and people in general than a child who is hugged, loved, approved, and nurtured does.

However, even with these extreme distinctions, parents who automatically implicate themselves in a grown child's failings and woes, or successes and joys, make a fundamental error. Although parents are absolutely responsible for how they treat their child, the child is absolutely responsible for how he or she adjusts to that treatment. Thus, the child of divorce is not responsible for the parental breakup but is responsible for his or her choice in adjusting to this difficult history.

This is why different adjustments can be made by different children in the same family to the same family event. One grown child looks back and says, "When my parents divorced, I lost all faith that loving relationships could ever last, so it's their fault that I have been distrustful of commitment ever since." Another grown child of the same divorce, however, comes away with a different choice for adjustment: "When my parents divorced, I was hurt and sorry for them, but I learned how important it is to communicate better in my relationships than they did in theirs." To the same adversity, people can make different choices for adjustment. This is why the child's responsibility for that adjustment must be respected. In any healthy relationship between parents and grown children, this division of responsibility needs to hold.

When parents blame their grown child's trials on themselves, they commit three errors:

1. They make a causative connection they cannot prove, as there are many variables in play that influence a young person's behavior.
2. They reduce their child's power of responsibility by encouraging him or her to hold them accountable for his or her choices.
3. They may open themselves up to manipulation of that guilt by their child, particularly when a young person is seeking rescue from consequences of a poor life choice.

I recall the parents of a twenty-two-year-old who described in counseling how they feel impelled to take responsibility for paying their daughter's credit card debts, because they never taught her how to manage money. "She says it's partly our fault," they confessed. "And she's right. We've always covered her expenses, no questions asked, so how else should we expect her to act?"

When parental guilt and a child's blame come together, the result can be mutually disabling—the parents take on too much responsibility, and the child does not take on enough. The resolution, of course, is for the parents to forsake their guilt by ceasing self-blame, and in the process emotionally disentangling the relationship. They need to be able to say to themselves, "How she conducts her life is not our fault; it is her choice."

So, for example, the parent listens empathetically to the young woman describing how frequent geographical moves—attending eight schools in twelve years—created instability in the family. It left her with anxiety when confronting further changes in her life, like the change she is facing upon graduating from college and stepping off on her own: "If my home had been stable I wouldn't lack the confidence that I feel now."

"Maybe so," agrees the father. "I know all those changes must have been pretty painful, and that some of that pain carries on in the insecurity you feel. I certainly take responsibility for creating the hard circumstances you describe, making so many job moves. But at this independent stage of your life, blaming family history for what feels hard only gets in the way of owning how you responded to these unhappy events. That is your responsibility to take. To free up your future, you must accept the family hand that you were dealt. How you play that hand is not up to what I did or didn't do; it's now up to you. You need to focus not on what I did but on what you want to do. My acting guilty and inviting further blame will only slow you down."

It is hard to be emotionally attached to your grown child and not become unhappily entangled with disappointment and guilt in the process. To avoid these burdens at the end of your child's adolescence means facing the hardest act of parenting there is— letting be and letting go. But that is what you have to do.

At the beginning of childhood, a stranger was born into your care. At the end of adolescence, an independent young adult departs from your care. In between these two events, a loving connection has been established that hopefully will sustain and nourish your relationship through the years ahead. A healthy parent– adult child connection requires having an adequate separation of responsibility, one that declares psychological independence between you both. When parents and child are both able to achieve independence, as a parent, you can honestly say and mean this:

"Our grown children are not meant to be ourselves, to repeat ourselves, to reflect ourselves, to affirm ourselves, to complete ourselves, to carry on ourselves, to repay ourselves, or to fulfill ourselves. They are simply meant to become themselves. And our job is to respect and accept and value them for the individuals they turn out to be."

RELATING TO THE ADULT CHILD

No matter how grown-up they become, your adult offspring for-ever remain your children, just as you forever remain their parent. And the relationship will always be challenging because, like the rest of life, parenting demands constant change and accommoda-tion. What makes this accommodation hard with adult children are several adjustments you must make: to tolerance, to reversal, and to demotion.

Let's start with *tolerance*. If you are in the sandwich generation, positioned between having older parents and adult children, you can learn to understand how your children sometimes still struggle with you by thinking about how you sometimes still struggle with your parents. You can see from becoming impatient with your own parents' ways how your adult children can get impatient with yours. You can recognize that when the values of one generation are discarded by the next, inevitable incompatibilities, conflict, and even estrangement can ensue. Intergenerational differences can be hard to tolerate.

Bridging these differences with acceptance, as you have learned to do with your own parents, is what you must learn to do with your grown children and what they must learn to do with you. You must lead the way. If you want them to accept your individual ways, you must accept their individual ways first. So you accept that you did not have perfect parents, that you were not a perfect parent yourself, and that your grown children were not and do not need to be perfect either. And you can hope they come to accept the imperfections in you. After all, at our best, all of us are only human.

Adjusting to *reversal* can be challenging as well. When the child is young, parents' task is to get the girl or boy to fit into their lives, to learn what they think is important, and to fulfill their agenda for what needs to happen. When the child becomes adult, however, to a significant degree, parents' roles reverse. Now the task is to fit more into the child's life, to understand what the grown daughter or son believes is important in life, to respect the adult child's agenda for what needs to happen, and to conduct the relationship more on her or his terms. Where once getting together meant the young person's coming to your home, now it more frequently entails your visiting them at their home.

Loss of traditional influence can be hard for some parents. In cases where parents still domineer their adult children or adult children still consent to submit, not daring to displease or challenge parental authority, it often takes bold acts of independence to break the situation. Sometimes for adult children this means waiting until their thirties to break this dependency. Then adult children stubbornly embrace a new life path, adopt a new lifestyle, or select a new life partner of whom parents disapprove. And when their parents question, criticize, or oppose this decision, the young people finally stand up for themselves with a defiant statement of independence: "It's my life, and I will live it as I please!" And now the old observation rings true: *"In the struggle over independence, parents never defeat their grown children; grown children always defeat their parents."*

The final reversal of the adult child–parent relationship plays out during the parents' older age, when the adult child begins taking care of the parent. Here the responsibility dramatically shifts, and the dependency reverses. At the beginning of childhood, the old take care and charge of their young; but at the end of parents' lives, the young take care and charge of their old.

The last adjustment parents must make in their relationship with their adult child is to accept their *demotion* in a child's life. When adult children become established in the world, preoccupation with managing their separate life can take precedence over being involved in parents' lives. When adult children marry, parents become less important than the new partner. And when adult children and their partners become parents, their parents become less important than the new child. Less important doesn't mean less loved, only less of a priority. As the adult child's life becomes more rich and complex, the role of parents becomes less central and more peripheral.

Then there can be the demotion from devoted to dutiful attention, when the weekly phone calls or occasional visits from an independent adult child, or remembering of special occasions, may feel more obligatory than heartfelt. But as one mother put it: "If dutiful is the best I can get, then I'll take it. Lesser caring is caring nonetheless."

This is the blessing and the curse of doing the job of parenting well. *When parents succeed in helping their children grow up to independence, these new adults will act more independently of them.*

So does parenting end with parents not mattering? Not at all, if parents remain mindful of their primary roles. Remember how your little child called "Watch me!" "Listen to me!" "See what I can do!" and "Let me tell you what I did!" What was it the little child wanted? The answer is parental attention, interest, and approval. These are needs the adult child never really outgrows. So when, as a parent, you continue your roles as emotional supporter, as rapt audience, and as tireless cheerleader, what you have to offer your adult children never goes out of style and never loses its lasting value.

Finally, as a goal for you and your grown child, consider how the German poet Rainer Maria Rilke described the optimal caring relationship in *Letters to a Young Poet*:

"Once the realization that even between the closest human beings infinite distances continue, a wonderful living side by side can grow, if they succeed in loving the distance between them which makes it possible for each to see the other whole against the sky."

PARENTING PRESCRIPTION

1. Accept that a mixed job of parenting is the best that you can do, and anticipate that your grown child will probably consider that flawed but full-faith effort good enough.

2. Create expectations that accept, and do not result in disappointment in, how your grown child turned out, and free both you and your grown child from the disabling entanglement of parental guilt and parent blame.

3. Treat your adult child by respecting differences between you, by relating more on the adult child's terms, and by accepting a demotion in traditional standing, and a loving relationship will come your way.

THE BENEFIT OF THE BOOMERANG EXPERIENCE

I wrote *Boomerang Kids* to help parents understand eleven life challenges that young people typically encounter upon leaving home for the final stage of adolescence, trial independence (ages 18–23). When any of these challenges comes to crisis, it can cause the young person to founder and boomerang home for sanctuary, for a time-out to recover and regroup before readying to leave and try independence once again.

Of the four adolescent stages that I describe, I believe the last, trial independence, is the hardest of all. Now young people are required to spread their wings and fly free of family, yet still find and keep a stable footing, and stay grounded, in a much larger and more demanding world than they anticipated.

And just as many young people were not fully prepared to leave and operate effectively on their own the first time out, most parents are unprepared to have them return. They thought their nest was empty and now suddenly it is full again—full of pressing needs and unresolved problems that have accompanied their son or daughter back home.

In fact, this temporary return is very common during the end of adolescence, and it creates an opportunity for parents to be of significant service to their returnee. By adopting a mentoring role, parents can be of enormous supportive and educational help. They can use their greater maturity to help their son or daughter turn adversity to advantage by mining the hardships encountered for the invaluable life lessons they have to teach.

At the same time, mentoring can strengthen the relationship between parents and their older adolescent with mutual appreciation, as parents respect the young person's right and responsibility to make independent decisions, and the young person respects the wisdom from life experience that parents have to offer.

SUGGESTED READING

Adams, Jane. *When Our Grown Kids Disappoint Us—Letting Go of Their Problems, Loving Them Anyway, Getting On with Our Lives.* New York: Free Press, 2003.

Arnett, Jeffrey Jensen. *Emerging Adulthood—The Winding Road from the Late Teens through the Twenties.* New York: Oxford University Press, 2004.

Arnett, Jeffrey Jensen, and Jennifer Lynn Tanner. *Emerging Adults in America—Coming of Age in the 21st Century.* Washington, D.C.: American Psychological Association, 2006.

Cote, James. *Arrested Adulthood—The Changing Nature of Maturity and Identity.* New York: New York University Press, 2000.

Furman, Elina. *Boomerang Nation—How to Survive Living with Your Parents...The Second Time Around.* New York: Fireside, 2005.

Guillamo-Ramos, Vincent, Jaccard, and Patricia Fittus. *Parental Monitoring of Adolescents*. New York: Columbia University Press, 2010.

Henig, Robin Marantz. "What Is It about 20-Somethings?" *New York Times Magazine*, August 22, 2010, p. 28.

Kadison, Richard, and Theresa Foy DiGeronimo. *College of the Overwhelmed—The Campus Mental Health Crisis and What to Do about It*. San Francisco: Jossey-Bass, 2004.

Mansfield, L. G. *Cutting the Cord—Eight Secrets to Coping When Your Kid Grows Sideways*. Nevada City, CA: Blue Fig Publishing, 2010.

Okimoto, Jean Davies, and Phyllis Jackson Stegall. *Boomerang Kids—How to Live with Adult Children Who Return Home*. New York: Pocket Books, 1987.

Pickhardt, Carl. *Stop the Screaming: How to Turn Angry Conflict with Your Child into Positive Communication*. New York: Palgrave Macmillan, 2009.

Pickhardt, Carl. *The Connected Father: Understanding Your Unique Role and Responsibilities During Your Child's Adolescence*. New York: Palgrave Macmillan, 2007.

Rilke, Rainer Maria. *Letters to a Young Poet*. Trans. Stephen Mitchell. New York: Vintage, 1986.

Settersten, Richard A., Jr., Frank F. Furstenberg Jr., and Ruben G. Rumbaut. *On the Frontier of Adulthood*. Chicago: University of Chicago Press, 2005.

Toffler, Alvin. *Future Shock*. New York: Random House, 1970.

INDEX

ABOUT THE AUTHOR

Carl Pickhardt, PhD, is a psychologist in a private counseling and public lecturing practice in Austin, Texas. He has four children and one grandchild. Pickhardt's books include *Why Good Kids Act Cruel*, *The Connected Father*, *The Future of Your Only Child*, *Stop the Screaming*, and many others.

He also writes a weekly blog for *Psychology Today*, Surviving (Your Child's) Adolescence. For more information about him and for a complete list of his books, see www.carlpickhardt.com